D1409017

Benjamin Fain

The Poverty of Secularism

An Open World Governed by the Creator versus a Closed, Imaginary World that Develops on Its Own

With a response to Richard Dawkins' *The God Delusion*

URIM PUBLICATIONS
Jerusalem • New York

The Poverty of Secularism: An Open World Governed by the Creator
versus a Closed, Imaginary World that Develops on Its Own
by Benjamin Fain

Translated from Hebrew by Karen Gilbert

Cover design, typesetting, and inside book design by
Jewish E-Books
www.jewish-e-books.com

Printed in Israel

ISBN-13: 978-965-524-136-5

Urim Publications
P.O. Box 52287, Jerusalem 91521 Israel

www.UrimPublications.com

CONTENTS

CHAPTER FOUR: THE CREATION OF THE WORLD AND ITS DEVELOPMENT

CHAPTER FIVE: THE HISTORY OF MAN

CHAPTER SIX: THE MEANING OF LIFE

PREFACE

Any living Judaism...will have to oppose pure naturalism with a definite no. It will have to insist that the currently so widespread notion of a world that develops out of itself and even is capable of independently producing the phenomenon of meaning – altogether the least comprehensible of all phenomena – can, to be sure, be maintained, but not seriously held.

(Gershom Scholem, *On Jews and Judaism in Crisis*, pp. 277-8)

Over time, and especially over the last few centuries, secularism has developed. *Secularism* is not a philosophy, ideology or movement, but the common denominator between different philosophies which are characterized by the *denial* of holiness and the negation of any connection to a deity in man's life. Movements and ideologies that differ widely in both purpose and content, such as communism, Nazism and western humanism, all regard themselves as secular. A secular thinker, even if he recognizes a deity, *denies* the idea that there is God's providence or involvement in the world and in the life of man.

The purpose of this book is to analyze various secular approaches and claims and to demonstrate their implausibility. That is, to show that secularism has no rational, scientific or philosophical basis. And in short, to expose the poverty of secularism.

Within modern man, who regards himself as enlightened and progressive, and as holding liberal views, there lies a deep, internal, philosophical contradiction. On the one hand, he believes in "scientific" materialism, which, in his mind, is supported by the great accomplishments of science, while on the other hand, human rights and freedoms are important to him and constitute an unshakable foundation of his social worldview. Modern man believes in the all-encompassing nature of physical causality, which is not compatible with human free will; however, in his day-to-day life as a member of society, free will is the most important element. It is impossible to protect the basic freedoms of man without attributing to him freedom of choice. Hence, free will should be at the foundation of modern man's moral outlook.

On the one hand, man is a product of nature. Secular philosophers view man as a sophisticated animal, a product of natural evolution – a totally materialistic process based on a combination of lawfulness and randomness. The conclusion that man's appearance as a result of evolution is meaningless and random is, therefore, inevitable. As the biologist G. G. Simpson writes in the Epilogue to his book, *The Meaning of Evolution*:

> Man is the result of a purposeless and materialistic process that did not have him in mind. He was not planned. He is state of matter, a form of life, a sort of animal, and a species of the order primates, akin nearly or remotely to all of life and indeed to all that is material.

(Needless to say, Simpson's claim that man "was not planned" is not derived from any scientific analysis.)

On the other hand, the secular view is characterized by a deep belief in the sovereignty of man – in his being at the center of the world, in a man-centered universe. It is man who gives meaning to the world, and it is man who determines the correct values and morals. According to Kant and his successors, man even determines the laws of nature, a subject which we will discuss in due course. Given this, there is a deep contradiction between the two tendencies in secularism: the deification of nature, that is, viewing nature as the source of everything (including the source of man), and the deification of man, that is, placing man at the center of the world. And these two cannot be reconciled.

The common notion held both by laymen and by those who see themselves, rightly or wrongly, as intellectuals and experts is that, from time immemorial, the world has been developing of its own accord and that science is able to describe and explain everything that exists in the world, including the human beings that live in it. Over time, science has developed, new horizons have opened up and science has been able to provide satisfactory explanations for phenomena that have previously remained a mystery. Modern physics is not a perfect science, and there are still many "gaps", but it is reasonable to assume that, with time, these "gaps" will also disappear.

According to the secular view, science develops and closes the gaps that remain. In contrast, religion focuses on things that science has not yet explained – on the "gaps" of science. If this is the case, then science develops, closes its gaps and hence the domain of religion shrinks. A phenomenon that today we do not understand and which appears to be a miracle will receive a scientific explanation tomorrow. The supporters of this worldview sometimes use the expression: "God of the Gaps". This God only exists because of people's ignorance: *necessary ignorance*, since science has not yet managed to solve all the problems, and *illiterate ignorance* which derives from a lack of knowledge of those issues that science has actually succeeded in explaining thus far.

It is important to understand that this kind of view is very commonly held these days, and can be called "scientific atheism" – atheism that is based, as it were, on the achievements of science. I see it as my duty to put forward an argument showing the utter unreasonableness of the secular viewpoint which seeks its legitimacy in the achievements of science. What is the answer to the expression "God of the Gaps", to the claim that as science develops it explains more and more new phenomena and shrinks the domain of religion? In due course we will see that there are many crucial subjects which are completely unrelated to science and which cannot be the subject of any scientific study. The claim that everything belongs to science and that therefore sooner or later all gaps will be closed, and that everything that is not currently understood will be explained by science in the future, is a wholly unscientific claim. On the contrary, we will see that the secular, naturalist, godless approach to creation and the development of the world is full of "gaps" which it is not capable of filling. It is not *God of the Gaps* but *Secularism with Gaps*! These gaps will not disappear while we are still clinging to a secular approach devoid of a living God. We will see that the world in which we live – including ourselves, human beings, as an important and inseparable part of it – cannot be explained or understood within the limitations and concepts of secularism.

To show this, we shall explore the essential realms of human culture such as *science, philosophy, ethics, cosmogony – the study of the formation of the universe – cosmology and theories of the development of life and humankind*. These subjects and others will be the objects of meticulous scrutiny intended to reveal the incompleteness and weaknesses of secularism. In light of this, it seems reasonable to begin our journey with a study of the structure of science and its limitations. In fact science is at the top of our agenda, but first we must talk about man. The appearance of man in this world and the phenomenon of man in general are the ultimate challenge for all worldviews and for secular philosophies in particular. This is why we should start our journey by contemplating man, his specialness and uniqueness, which cannot be compared with any other phenomenon known to us.

To avoid any potential misunderstanding, I would like to stress that my arguments are not directed against people who are considered to be secular or who call themselves "secular"; they are directed against the worldview to which they adhere. Everyone is judged according to his own actions; a person may be exposed to brainwashing in various periods of his life, and nevertheless he may do good deeds, to the point of self-sacrifice, since his soul is aware of its internal connection with God. In any case, the distinction between religious people and secular people is not clear-cut and it is also not accepted from a religious point of view. Various sociological studies conducted in Israel have shown that there is no sharp divide between the religious and the non-religious. In fact, amongst up to eighty per cent of the population there is a broad spectrum of different levels of religious consciousness and observance.

A few words about the name of the book. Karl Marx wrote a book called *The Poverty of Philosophy*, in which he responded to Proudhon's *The Philosophy of Poverty*. Karl Popper, in turn, wrote *The Poverty of Historicism*, which is a play on Marx's title. I have decided to call my book *The Poverty of Secularism*. Just like two of the books mentioned here which contain a critique of a particular worldview or outlook, this book also includes a critique of the worldview that is based on the denial of holiness and of any connection to the divine in the life of man.

In addition to the critical part of the book that is intended to show the poverty of secularism, there is also a more positive section which relates to the Jewish-religious worldview as an alternative to secularism. However, the critical analysis is not in any way dependent on this or any other alternative view. In the positive part of the book I have used ideas that were brought in my previous books, *Creation Ex Nihilo* and *Law and Providence*. This book contains a summary of those ideas and develops them somewhat, but anyone keen to delve into the subject of Torah and science would benefit from reading these two books. It is worth mentioning that the use of the Jewish view as an alternative to secularism is not exclusive to the author's Judaism. Four thousand years ago the most important ideological revolution in the history of man began – the Torah was revealed to humankind and the biblical worldview began to spread across the world. This worldview was also the ideological basis of religions that were founded later on – Christianity and Islam. Hence, the use of Judaism as an alternative to secularism has a universal dimension that is shared with these religions too.

* * *

I would like to express my gratitude to the first readers of the manuscript of this book (the Hebrew original). To my wife, Shoshana, for her wonderful support and valuable comments; to Dr. Daniel Shalit and Yehudit Rachmani for their helpful remarks and observations. I would also like to thank Efrat Lieber for her tireless work as linguistic editor of the Hebrew version of this book. This book is a translation from the Hebrew of my book *Dalut ha'Kfirah*. I would like thank the translator, Karen Gilbert, for her fruitful cooperation.

CHAPTER ONE: MAN – MYSTERY OF MYSTERIES

Man sees the thing that surround him long before he becomes
aware of his own Self. Many of us are conscious of the hiddenness
of things, but few of us sense the mystery of our own presence. The
self cannot be described in terms of the mind, for all our symbols
are too poor to render it.

(Abraham Joshua Heschel, *The Wisdom of Heschel*, p. 124)

The routine of day-to-day life prevents us from gaining a deep
understanding of the reality in which we live. The world is full
of divine revelations but we have difficulty seeing them. Modern
man has been educated on the basis that everything in the world is material and natural, and that there is no room for anything supernatural. And
most importantly, the world is scientific. Every phenomenon in the world
can be scientifically described and explained, and if there are things that
have not yet been explained by science, then that is just a temporary situation, and sooner or later science will explain these too. We learn this from
the progress of science: in the past there were many things that were not
understood, and eventually science has explained them. If this is the case,
then thus it shall be in the future as well – what we do not comprehend
today we will understand tomorrow, thanks to the development of science. There are no, and nor can there be any, mysteries in the world, and
if something seems to us to be a mystery, tomorrow science will explain
it and the riddle will be solved.

This view, which has thrived against the backdrop of the incredible accomplishments of science, is nothing but a unfounded preconception. The claim that everything in the world, including the world itself and its development, belong solely to science is not true. In due course we will devote specific chapters to this subject and we will discuss science in detail, but at this point I will mention that by its very nature science is only capable of describing things that exist in multiple copies and recurring events. In short, science belongs to the public domain. There is order and lawfulness in the world, and science describes them. It can precisely predict the future movements of the heavenly bodies, such as a solar eclipse in the twenty-second century, or the trajectories of macroscopic bodies such as ballistic missiles. Science can also describe the attributes and the laws of the tiniest particles – the *microcosmos* – the world of quantum particles. All this leads to a sense of the omnipotence and omniscience of science.

However, science is incapable of answering questions such as: Where does the order and lawfulness in the world come from? How is it that the laws of nature uniform throughout Earth as well as on the most distant stars? Science is not even capable of solving far simpler problems, such as predicting the behavior of a cat. Furthermore, there are no scientific tools that can predict the precise path of a cat in the next few moments, even when we have the maximum amount of information possible about the cat and its environment at a particular point in time. This is in contrast to the prediction of the precise paths of the heavenly bodies, hundreds of years into the future. In general, the *purposeful* behavior of animals, such as searching for food, makes it very difficult for there to be a scientific explanation for their actions. The world in which we live is far richer and more diverse than being limited to a Procrustean bed solely of scientific explanation. The mistaken assumption that everything can be described and explained scientifically makes it difficult for us to discern the wonderful and mysterious aspects of reality. But we will discuss this further in due course.

The world is full of wonders that our routine and our preconceptions prevent us from seeing. But let us not look far afield for the wonders of the world; let us focus on the phenomenon of *man*. The routine of our daily lives and the routine of our thought prevents us from seeing the greatest miracle in our world, a miracle that we live with each and every moment. This miracle, this wonder, is *man*. Let us start with the fact that man is the most complex and sophisticated creature in the world. He is more complex than the solar system, and than all the stars and galaxies put together. But this does not give us even the slightest concept of his complexity, since even a tiny fly is more complex that all the galaxies. People's bodies are extremely similar to each other (differences in the genetic code from one person to the next are miniscule, approximately 0.01%) and therefore the human body is in the public domain and can be the subject of scientific research. This is the case when we are talking about the human *body*, organs that are made of matter. Anything that human beings are capable of building, such as sophisticated computers, does not come close to the complexity of the human body.

The human body is differentiated from the bodies of other developed species, such as primates, only quantitatively, but man has something else which belongs exclusively to him. Man has a *soul* that feels and is aware of his *Self*. In order to understand what these words mean, we must take a look at ourselves. We can all do this. Since my early childhood up to the present day I have felt and experienced my Self. I feel the Self in an immediate and unmediated way. I do not need any proofs, neither logical nor experimental, for the existence of my Self. The reality of my Self is primary for me, and I grasp the world outside of me by my intellect, through my Self. This is not a metaphysical-philosophical claim but a fact of life. Everything that happens in the world, all the events in my life and in the lives of my friends and family – it is all captured in my consciousness by my Self, as a part of its internal experience. When I observe my Self after a period of time in which I have been unconscious – asleep or under a general anesthetic – I wake up and determine that my Self has not changed. Likewise, when I look at my life and the important moments of it, I come to the conclusion that there is *continuity* of my Self. My child-Self and my adult-Self are the same Self. *I have no doubt about the reality and certainty of my Self.*

Like all people, I have a variety of different *emotions*, such as love, friendship, jealousy and resentment, and sometimes I feel *pain* and I am capable of *thinking* about various things. I have been involved in science my whole life; I have written and published books in various fields of physics and I have achieved a number of *intellectual accomplishments*. Why am I saying all this? Because none of these – emotions, thoughts, pains, intellectual accomplishments – are connected to matter, nor are they connected to the material of my body. These are spiritual things, characteristics of the *spiritual entity*, of my soul. Hence, by looking inwards, I have come to the wonderful conclusion that I am not only physical but I also have within me *spirit*.

The insight that the soul is a spiritual entity is a very important one. Modern man, who sees himself as an educated and enlightened person, identifies a thing's "realness" with its objective materiality, and as far as he is concerned spiritual entities are subjective, and therefore they are not real. In fact, there is no way to imagine, describe or explain a spiritual entity in scientific terms that are intended to describe objects made of matter. Even if we ignore the problem of explaining a spiritual thing, the very existence of a spiritual entity is extremely difficult to understand. People tend to regard those who refuse to identify reality with materiality as mystics, but this is simply an unfounded notion. In the past no scientific explanation was considered plausible if it did not contain a sufficient degree of "tangibility"; take, for example, Newton's general law of gravity which was associated with the falling apple. In contrast, in modern physics even ordinary matter can be explained using symbols alone. What is this reminiscent of? It is reminiscent of Jewish mysticism (*Kabbalah*), which also makes extensive use of symbols.

Acknowledgment of the fact that I am composed of – if the term "composed of" is actually appropriate here – two entities, material and spiritual, is not at all simple, and perhaps even impossible. *It is very difficult to discern the wondrous and the mysterious in our day-to-day experience. The human soul is one of the mysteries of the world.* We can take, as an analogy, a child who is used to the reality of television and does not see anything special in it at all. He will need to grow up and learn a great deal in order to understand how it works. This analogy is limited, however, by the fact that television can be studied and understood using scientific means, while my inner world, my Self, does not belong to the realm of science at all. As we have already mentioned, science cannot describe things and events that do not belong to the public domain, that are unique. But everyone is unique. We have said that the human body belongs to the public domain, but man's soul is special and unique. It is both spiritual and unique and perhaps these are not two different qualities. Ultimately all creations are spiritual.

It takes great intellectual effort to shake off the childish outlook that accepts day-to-day routine as self-evident. Let us take a look at various types of machines, at a car or a state-of-the-art computer, for example. What these have in common is that the machine is always operated by a person. These days, biologists "determine" that the human brain is similar to a state-of-the-art, highly sophisticated computer, but no machine or computer can operate itself. Somebody needs to navigate the car or the airplane; someone has to program the computer, operate it and read its output. Here we come to the critical point, which requires great intellectual effort to free ourselves of the restraints of our routine thinking. My brain has a master, who programs and operates it, and that master is the Self. The mystery lies in the fact that I have no tools with which to describe the Self and the manner in which it operates the body and the brain . We are used to the fact that everything in the world, such as machines, biological organs and the brain can be described using scientific tools, and we are used to the fact that all these things are made of matter. We must extricate ourselves from this routine way of thinking and realize that there is a mystery here. The Self is a spiritual entity, and it uses the brain, as its own personal computer.

In fact, in a way it is "easier" to know the soul than it is to know the body – since a person's thoughts and feelings need no proof, while he knows his body only through inquiry and learning. Two eminent researchers of the twentieth century, Karl Popper and John Eccles, wrote a book entitled *The Self and Its Brain*. The book does not address the problem with which we are grappling, but takes it as a given that the *spirit* operates the brain and through it, the entire body. How? The authors intentionally ignore questions of this kind. There is something that is not biological, that is not material – and it is the *Self*, which uses the human body (and brain).

Looking at the history of western philosophy, René Descartes (1596-1650) is someone who differentiates between two different entities or between two substances: the substance represented by the physical world, which Descartes called "the substance that extends in space", and "the thinking substance", which is represented by man's consciousness. It is worth pointing out that the idea of the two substances, body and soul, which have a reciprocal, interactive relationship, has a long-standing tradition in Jewish thought. In fact, Descartes also drew his ideas from his religious tradition which included the Bible.

In the first verses of the Book of Genesis, we read: "And the Lord God formed man out of the dust of the ground, and breathed into his nostrils the breath of life; and man became a living soul." Nachmanides, the eminent Jewish philosopher and commentator who lived in the thirteenth century (1194-1270), explains this: "And the verse says that He breathed into his nostrils the breath of life in order to inform us that the soul did not come to man from the elements...Rather it was the spirit of the Great God: out of his mouth comes knowledge and discernment. For he who breathes into the nostrils of another person gives into him something from his own soul." (*Nachmanides' Commentary on the Torah*, Genesis 2:7). God gives man a part of his soul, so to speak. Nachmanides continues: "and the whole man became a living soul since by virtue of this soul he understands and speaks and does all his deeds..." Onkelos translates the words "living soul", the soul that apparently characterizes every living being as "talking spirit", and emphasizes the uniqueness of man. Following him, Rashi explains: "Cattle and beasts were also called living souls, but this one of man is the most alive of them all, because he was additionally given intelligence and speech." Rabbi Soloveitchik summarizes: "a spark of the Creator is concealed in him" – in man. This spark exists within the *Self* of each of us.

Now we come to the extra aspect of the wonder of man – there is interaction between the human body and soul, and they affect one another. How do we know this? How do I know this? From my personal experience, just as each of us knows it from his own personal experience. We have already learned that the human body is a highly complex, sophisticated and delicate mechanism. How do I operate it? What must be done so that the human body gets out of bed after a sleep, so that it turns left or right, so that it moves, so that it drives, so that it does any number of other physical actions? I, my *Self*, need only to *decide* which action to do. This is not an explanation for the interaction between body and soul; it is simply a statement of its existence. Mutual influence between a body and a spiritual entity is indeed an amazing thing, but cannot be explained using terminology from the world of matter; there cannot be a *scientific* explanation for it. We remain steeped in wonder. Regarding the great difficulty in comprehending the interaction between the body and the soul, Nachmanides writes: "A material thing [man] cannot fully comprehend how the separate entity [the intellect, which is spiritual rather than physical] can affect this physical reality..." Even though man is an intelligent being, and can understand many things, there is one thing that is beyond his comprehension: How can a *spiritual entity* be an active agent in the physical reality?

Approximately three hundred years after Nachmanides, Rabbi Moshe Isserles, who wrote a commentary on the Shulchan Aruch, interprets the wondrous nature of the connection between body and mind. The blessing "who fashioned man with wisdom..." talks about man's body and its physical functions. The blessing ends with the words: "Blessed are you, God, Who heals all flesh and acts wondrously". After this comes one of the most sublime prayers to be found in the prayer book, which opens with the words: "My God, the soul you placed within me is pure", after which come the blessings of the Torah, which bring us to the world of the spirit. The words "acts wondrously" stand between the two worlds – between the reference to bodily functions and the reference to the life of the spirit and the mind. What is Rabbi Moshe Isserles' interpretation? Acts wondrously, in what? According to the structure of the prayer book, it seems that these words refer to the part that comes before them, to the biological functions. One could also say, in accordance with what comes after these words, that they also relate to the great wonder of the psychic reality of mankind. But Rabbi Moshe Isserles says that *the wonder is the connection between the two things.* The fact that two entities – body and soul – are connected to one another, is difficult to comprehend even for a person who believes that both the world of nature and the world of the spirit were created by God. *He acts wondrously* – He connects a spiritual entity with a physical entity – *that is the wonder.*

Here we come to a great mystery, perhaps even greater than those already mentioned: the possibility of free will. It is this that differentiates man from the rest of the world, from the inanimate world, from plants and from animals. The entire world, apart from man, acts according to the necessity that is determined by the laws of nature, including the controlling instincts in the animal world. Everything in the world complies with the same laws, but only man has free will. However, instincts also influence man, but only man has the ability to overcome them and to decide to act contrary to them. Man is capable of deciding not to obey even God's command. Thanks to man's free will, he is able to create new spiritual things. The huge mass of creations that mankind has produced over the course of its existence is brought together in the collective memory of all human beings – the culture of mankind. Every person has the wonderful ability to connect to this spiritual world, and to introduce into his own memory a part of the collective memory of humanity. Because of the routine of our daily lives we accept this incredible quality as a given – the ability to participate in other people's religious experiences, to use different languages, to experience great musical pieces from the past, to master impressive scientific works – namely to connect to the spiritual world of another person, even if that person lived hundreds or thousands of years previously. Of the entire living world only man has this wonderful ability.

We have before us a special creature and it is only our routine way of thinking that prevents us from realizing it. Man is the most complex and sophisticated creature in the world from a physical perspective, but what is truly amazing about him is that he is combined with spirit, with a spiritual entity that controls him and determines his behavior. And most importantly, that he has free will and is capable of overcoming the necessity of the laws of nature and his own animal instincts.

Now let us ask ourselves this: How can such a complex, sophisticated and wonderful creature, one that belongs both to the world of the spirit and the world of matter, be created? This question seems a little odd. It is clear that there must be a creator for the creation. It is clear that no creation, not even the simplest of creations, can be created "by itself", without someone creating it. When we come across a particular text, whether it is in the library or from an archeological dig, it does not even occur to us to deny the existence of a creator, of an author of the text, even for the simplest of texts. It would seem all the more clear that there must be a creator for a creation as complex as man. This is what simple intellect teaches us, and this is also what our accumulated experience teaches us. Throughout the entire history of humanity there has not been even one instance of the formation of a creation by itself, without a creator.[1]

Nonetheless there is a preconception that man was formed from nature, or to be more precise, that nature itself created man, and that science has proved this. Let us try to understand what we are talking about here. A very long time ago there were no living creatures in the world, just primary raw matter. There was just inanimate nature and its laws. Nature developed according to these laws, and as it developed it "created" new entities, such as different animals, and the pinnacle of its creation was man, which itself creates numerous other creations. And apparently this entire huge project can be described using scientific tools. According to this, no creator is required here – nature itself creates everything, including man. This secular worldview is based, as it were, on the achievements of science. This picture of the world is accepted by very many people, both scientists in various fields and laymen who rely on those scientists. This view is considered to be a substitute for the religious worldview

---

1. Of course, I am aware of David Hume's argument in *Dialogues Concerning Natural Religion*, that there is no analogy between the person-creator and God. But there is also no analogy between man's creations and divine creations. My main argument is that a creation as complex as man cannot be created without a creator.

which is supposedly outdated. This is what is claimed by the adherents of atheism, who are convinced that there was no need for any creator for the creations of the world, and even for the creation of the world itself. But it is not true that the atheistic worldview is based on and supported by science, and that there are scientific proofs for the creation of man by nature. There are no such proofs, and nor can there be any. We will see this in due course, *and this is, in fact, one of the aims of this book.*

According to the Torah, too, the world was only raw matter at the start: "And the earth was without form and void, and darkness was on the face of the deep" (Genesis 1:2) and man was created from that matter – "dust of the ground". But the major difference between this and the secular explanation is that the earth itself did not create man, God created him: "And the Lord God formed man of the dust of the ground" (Genesis 2:7). It is worth pointing out that the Torah is not concerned with explaining and detailing how the divine plan was carried out, how man was formed – all at once or in a gradual, evolutionary process. The point is that it was not nature, or the ground, but rather it was God that created him. The secular view, that matter – nature – is the source of all things, including human beings and their creations, is actually a kind of idol worship, a deification of nature. The Torah mentions this explicitly: "and has gone and served other gods, and worshipped them, either the sun, or moon, or any of the host of heaven, which I have not commanded" (Deuteronomy 17:3).

We have before us two diametrically opposed worldviews. One is based on the Torah, divine revelation, straightforward intellect and accumulated human experience, while the other is irrational, going against both intellect and experience but claiming to be scientific, that is, supported by science. As we have mentioned, this claim is not true, and later on I shall prove it. As I have stated, according to this worldview, nature itself has formed many diverse creations, it has also created man and it is the source of man's creations. This view is very commonly held in the western world, and the soviet regime even included it in its official ideology. Therefore it is very important to understand the weakness and the deficiencies of this belief, which is a modern form of idolatry.

The points discussed in this chapter can serve as an introduction to the discussion of the value and meaning of the secular worldview. Or, to be more precise, of the ideological foundation of different secular philosophies. *The question that we need to answer is whether there is actually any scientific basis to the claim that nature or matter are capable of forming, by themselves – without any external agent, without a creator – different creations, and in particular a grand, complex and sophisticated creation such as man?* As we have mentioned, the answer will be unequivocal: *There is no scientific basis to the claim that nature itself creates things, including man.* To this end we will need to study the nature, structure and limitations of science. The next chapter shall be devoted to this.

CHAPTER TWO: THE LAWS OF NATURE-SCIENCE

1. The Laws of Nature[1]

"How great are Your works, O Lord, You have made them all with wisdom; the earth is full of Your possessions."

Psalms 104:24

In the previous chapter we came to the conclusion that the claim that a creature as complex and sophisticated as man was created by itself from the raw matter of the universe is not compatible with common sense and with the accumulated experience of humanity. There is no experience that indicates that any thing has come into the world without someone having created it, and this is all the more absurd when we are talking about man. This conclusion is compatible with common sense and our accumulated experience. Regarding the opposite claim – that man was formed spontaneously from nature as it developed – there is no rational or scientific basis to this claim, though because this is such a widely held view, we will discuss it in detail later on, in the chapters about the development of the world. According to the Jewish-religious worldview, there is a rational basis to everything that is in the world and to the world itself – there is a superior intellect. In contrast, according to the materialist approach, the source of everything is matter that is devoid of any intelligence or spirituality, and we are also a random consequence of that material, reason-less source.

---

1. I hope that I will succeed in this section to bring to the reader some basic concepts of modern physics. If parts of this section seem too complicated, the reader should feel free to skip them and move on to the next part.

In the previous chapter we looked at the wonder that is man, who, according to the secular argument, was created by nature itself, without any external force. In this chapter we will talk about nature without man. Both according to the Torah and according to science there was an initial, fairly lengthy, period in which man did not yet exist and nor were there any animals or plants, just inanimate objects. Even today, the inanimate world fills most of the volume of the universe, and in fact, we know nothing about the existence of life anywhere other than on Earth. In this chapter we will focus on the raw material from which all physical objects, including the human body, are made, and we will talk about nature and its laws. However, it is important to understand that reading this chapter, as with other parts of this book, has a clearly defined goal: to provide food for thought for our "evolving" discussion on secularism, which will be continued at the end of each section.

The field of human knowledge that describes, explains and analyzes the laws of nature and their implications is science, or, to be more precise, *physics*. We first come across the word *physics* with the philosopher Aristotle. Aristotle, who lived in Ancient Greece in 384-322 BCE, dealt in great detail with the problem of motion. It should be noted that Greece at that time was considered the center of philosophy and mathematics. It would not be an exaggeration to say that at the dawn of modern science, in the sixteenth century, the level of knowledge in the area of mathematics and nature was more or less equal to that of Ancient Greece. So Galileo, who was born in 1564 and is considered a pioneer of modern science, learned mathematics and nature from the works of Euclid and Archimedes. Aristotle wrote numerous works of philosophy (back then no distinction was made between philosophy and science), which had great influence on many generations after him, and in particular in the Middle Ages. One of his books was called *Physics*. Thus the word that denotes the science of matter was born.

What characterizes modern physics, and modern science in general, is their strong connection with experiment. Scientific theories are tested by experiments, and it is from here that their quantitative nature is derived. Scientific theories, and physics in particular, are formulated and expressed in the *language of mathematics*. Ordinary human languages, such as English, French or Hebrew are not capable of describing the laws of nature and the various natural phenomena.

Many mathematical concepts have already penetrated our language, even if we are unaware of it. There are some primitive languages which only include the concepts *one*, *two* and *many*. Clearly languages of this kind are not able to express complex connections between certain groups of objects. In primitive languages such as these, one can say that in one flock there are more sheep than there are in the second flock, but one cannot express the fact that in the first flock there are 34 sheep, which is three more than in the second flock. *In other words, mathematical symbols entered language in order to describe complex relationships that could not be described otherwise.* A language that contains arithmetic, natural numbers, is richer than a language that does not contain these symbols.

In general one might say that for a deeper understanding of reality a richer language is required. Without a doubt, modern science has succeeded in attaining a very deep understanding of the material reality. Physical theories describe different aspects of reality in such a complex way that laymen are not able to grasp them at all, in precisely the same way that speakers of a more primitive language are incapable of grasping things that can only be described using a language that contains arithmetic. Similarly, a language that includes modern mathematics, the fruits of thousands of years of development, is capable of describing a far more complex and sophisticated reality than that which can be described by speakers of a weak (ordinary) language which does not incorporate modern mathematics.

And herein lies the difference: the language that we speak has included arithmetic and other mathematical concepts for a long time. We have become accustomed to this, and we no longer pay attention to it. However, modern mathematics has not entered our spoken language, but is the property of an extremely small group of scientists and mathematicians. But this does not change the fact that mathematics constitutes a part of the general human language, even though most people still do not understand it.

In light of this, we can understand the difficulty in explaining the structure of nature and its development. An appropriate description of nature, the description given by modern physics, can only be expressed with the mathematical tools used by physics. Nevertheless, we can state some general characteristics of nature and its laws. Physics uses particular mathematical symbols to express the laws of nature, and generally it is impossible to translate these symbols into ordinary language. But the most important characteristic of science is that there has to be a connection between these symbols and the results of the experiment. As we have said, science is characterized by the fact that its theoretical ramifications can always be tested by experiment. For example, science might predict that on a particular date in the future there will be a solar eclipse. Obviously, this solar eclipse can only be tested when that date arrives.

Physics describes the laws of nature using mathematical equations. These equations reflect the attributes of the laws of nature – they apply to all physical objects, everywhere in the world, and they determine their development over time. Objects or physical systems develop over time according to the stipulations of the law, while the law itself does not change and is not dependent on time or the object's location in space.

Hence, for an infinite number of possible movements – each with their own unique initial conditions – the same law of nature applies and the same mathematical equations express that law. One could say that a law

Initial Conditions

Here is another important aspect of physical lawfulness. There are numerous, in fact infinite, solutions to the mathematical equation that expresses a law of nature. What do I mean by this? The equation that expresses the law of nature does not exclusively determine the movement of the physical objects, the movement of matter. Look at Figure 1, which is taken from one of Isaac Newton's works. At point V, different objects are launched in the same

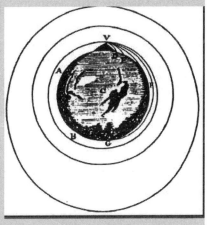

Figure 1. Objects are thrown from point V on Earth at different speeds

direction but at different initial speeds. After the object is sent off it is subject to Earth's gravitational field. The first object, at a relatively low speed, lands at point D, the closest point to the point of launch. The second object, at a higher speed, falls at point E. The object with an even higher starting speed comes to rest at point F, which is even farther away.

It is interesting that there is a speed at which an object traveling at it would not fall to the ground at all, but would instead become a kind of satellite. From a mathematical perspective, all of these paths are solutions of the mathematical equation that expresses a particular law of nature. These paths are dependent not only on the law of nature (the mathematical equation), but also on the initial conditions – the speed and the point of launch. A particular law, therefore, includes an infinite number of possible movements for different initial positions. The laws of science do not provide the initial conditions; only experiment enables them to be determined.

of nature is an entity that does not change with the transition from one path to another, from one initial condition to another. A law of nature is fixed – there are numerous, infinite possible paths, which "comply with" the same law. However, it is crucial to understand that the law of nature is also *preserved* within one particular path, in each one of the paths. What do I mean by this? The path of a particular physical object describes the development of that object over time – at every moment it is in another location and is traveling at a different speed. The position of the object is dependent on time, but the law of nature itself does not change – it is fixed and is not dependent on time. We can conclude that the law of nature is fixed in two ways: (a) it is fixed and does not change from one path to another; (b) it is fixed within the development of the physical system in time – the system changes with the passage of time but the law of nature does not change. We can also state this as follows: All the physical objects in the world (the physical systems) comply with the same law of nature (or the same laws of nature), with the law of nature unchanging, fixed, for the entire duration of the development of the system.

Physics deals with the lawfulness of nature on two distinct planes – the macroscopic plane and the microscopic plane. We are very familiar with the macroscopic plane. This is everything we see around us – buildings, cars, tables etc, as well as the heavenly bodies, stars, galaxies and the like. We are talking about large blocks of matter that can be seen by the naked eye. Things that we can see and feel. In contrast, microscopic systems cannot be seen or felt, and in many cases they cannot even be imagined. These are atoms and molecules, fundamental, elementary particles, such as electrons and protons, and sub-elementary particles such as quarks and strings[2].

From a historical perspective, macroscopic systems have been the subject of scientific research from the dawn of science. More than three centuries ago Isaac Newton formulated the fundamental laws of mechanics and the law of gravity; in the second half of the nineteenth century James Clerk Maxwell discovered and devised the electro-magnetic field theory; and at the start of the twentieth century Albert Einstein, with

---

2.   The reader does not need to be familiar with these terms.

his special and general theory of relativity, completed the magnificent corpus of classical physics. Also at that time, at the start of the twentieth century, it became clear that the scope of classical physics was limited to macroscopic systems, to large blocks of matter, while for a description of the microcosmos, the world of the micro (miniscule), another approach is required, one that is different from that of classical physics. Thus quantum physics was born, to which Einstein also made a significant contribution by setting out its foundations. But before we discuss quantum physics, we should provide a brief overview of the main points of classical physics.

What characterizes classical physics is the fact that it is *deterministic*. This means that the laws of the macrocosmos unequivocally determine all the future development of the system. Furthermore, it is also possible to reconstruct its past, as long as we know all about the system at a particular time in the present or the past. These laws are described by the equations of classical physics. Different solutions to these equations describe different movements (with different initial conditions) of different physical (macroscopic) objects. One concept that belongs to the deterministic world is *causality* – the same cause gives rise to the same effect. The laws of nature connect the cause and the effect. Thus, for example, throwing a stone causes it to fall. The law of nature that connects the throw and the fall is the law of gravity; every object that is thrown upwards is pulled towards the ground by the gravitational force. It should be noted that philosophers, both past and present, quite often apply the laws of physics to everything in the world and claim that the world is deterministic – that everything is pre-determined, and that general causality prevails in our world – everything has a cause, and the same cause leads to the same effect. However, it is important to remember that the laws of physics are only a reflection of the laws of nature – of the real laws that prevail in the world; and this reflection is generally only valid at a certain approximation.

As we have mentioned, classical physics is not the whole truth but only an approximation to the truth. When talking about the particles of which blocks of matter are made, these particles "obey" the quantum laws, the main feature of which is that they are not deterministic. This means that the quantum laws do not unequivocally determine what is going to happen with a quantum system in the future, even if we have the maximum information possible on the position of the system at a particular point in time. Quantum theory provides only probabilities – likelihoods – for possible eventualities that may happen in the quantum system. For example, if an atom is in an excited state (i.e. a state of high energy) it may emit light, or to be more precise, it may emit a photon, the smallest unit of light. Quantum theory is capable of predicting that sooner or later the atom will emit a photon, but it is not able to predict when this will happen. Quantum theory is only able to provide a distribution of probabilities that the atom will emit a photon at one time or another. However, when we are talking about a single atom, probabilities do not help, as they can only be tested in a large group of atoms. In other words, between the cause – an atom in an excited state – and the result – the emission of a photon – there is a loose, indefinite connection. The photon will be emitted, but there is no law that can determine the time of emission. Thus the predictions of quantum theory do not determine the future in a definitive, unequivocal way.

We will now focus on the qualities of matter, any matter, from a quantum perspective. Classical physics has succeeded in describing the movements of classical objects, but the essence of objects, blocks of matter, is an enigma for classical physics. Only quantum physics provides consistent theories of matter, whether solid, liquid or gas, and whether molecules, atoms or elementary particles. It is not our goal here to explain these theories, but we should discuss their fundamental concepts, the basic entities of which matter is composed.

Every physical object contains a physical field or *physical fields,* and *elementary particles.* These entities are not at all similar to what we encounter in our day-to-day lives. Here I should add a few words about terminology. We spoke above about matter, about blocks of matter. Everyone knows (or thinks they know) what matter is. Matter is a rock, a chair, a table, our limbs. Matter is everything that is defined in space (and this includes liquids and gases). One can see, feel, push and be pushed by a material object. In contrast, the physical field, a term that we will discuss later, is a physical entity which we generally do not see or feel, and which is not limited, but spreads out across the entire area.

A Static Electrical Field

On the left side of the diagram we can see a "picture" of an electrical field with a positive charge (+) (in the center of the diagram). The arrows show the forces at

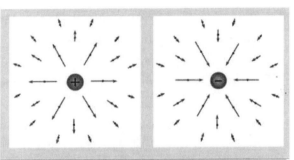

Figure 2: Electrical fields

(Right) Field of negative electrical charge

(Left) Field of positive electrical charge

various points of the field. All the arrows point outwards from the central charge. This means that if you place a positive electrical charge at a particular point, a force will act on it repelling it from the central charge. The length of the arrow in the diagram shows the relative size of the force. We can see that the length of the arrow decreases as the distance from the central charge increases, which reflects the fact that the electrical forces diminish as their distance from the central charge increases. On the right side of the diagram we see an electrical field with a negative charge (−). It is attracted to positive charges and hence all the arrows point inwards, towards the charge.

Now let us try to understand what a physical field is. Today physics recognizes various types of physical fields, but Maxwell's theory of electromagnetism was the first to bring to physics a consistent and detailed theory of the physical field – the electromagnetic field. In addition, the electromagnetic field is present in our lives in such a constant way, that we can hardly imagine ourselves without the electromagnetic devices that surround us, such as electric lights, radio, television, microwaves and the like. How can we define the field using concepts that we can understand? Let us look, for example, at the fields of electrical charges, positive and negative (Figure 2).

An electrical charge, positive or negative, creates an electrical field (static, which is not dependent on time) in the space around it. In contrast to a material object which is concentrated in a particular place with a particular volume, an electrical field takes up all of the space. What does it mean that an electrical field exists in every point in space? An electrical field is a field of electrical forces. An electrical force acts on an electrical charge if it is situated at a particular point in space. A certain degree of abstraction is required to grasp the fact that an electrical field exists even in a space that has no charges (outside of the charge that creates the field – the central charge in the diagram). At every point in the area the forces of the field exist, even if there are no charges in the area on which the forces are acting. In order to test whether an electrical force exists at a particular point, an electrical charge must be placed at that point, and then we will see that the electrical field will repel or attract it in the direction of the charge creating the field: $(+)$ or $(-)$ as in Figure 2.

I am sitting in my room. It contains all kinds of material items, but in addition it also contains electromagnetic fields, electromagnetic waves at various frequencies (various wavelengths). To some extent, we are able to "see" optical electromagnetic waves in the visible range. Light from the sun or from electric lights is comprised of electromagnetic waves of this type. In my room there are also electromagnetic waves in the radio range. It is impossible to see or to feel these waves. However, one can receive radio waves using radio receivers and shorter waves can be received using television sets. Similarly, in the visible range, our seeing devices, including our eyes, perceive the presence of the electromagnetic field.

Now let us take a look at another physical entity, the second component of matter, the *elementary particles*. While the physical field exists in classical physics, elementary particles are a quantum entity. The classical theory cannot deal with atoms or molecules, with crystals or their components – elementary particles. Elementary particles, and the entities that are composed of them, such as atoms and molecules, are *quantum* objects. If it was difficult to describe and explain what a physical field is, it is impossible to imagine or explain quantum objects at all, since they are not like anything with which we are familiar. The word particle is misleading. There is no similarity between a quantum particle and particles with which we are familiar in our daily lives – very tiny pieces of matter, such as grains of sand.

A quantum particle has both particle-like and wave-like properties. If we try to study it, to conduct experiments on it, it will become apparent that in some experiments it behaves like a classic particle while in other experiments it behaves like a wave – something which cannot be illustrated or visualized. The concept of a wave always refers to things that are spread out, such as a water wave or an airwave. While a classic particle is concentrated in one point, a wave does not have defined borders and it occupies a wide area. There is no point in expanding here on the strange and counter-intuitive properties of quantum objects, such as having both particle-like and wave-like properties. But it does raise the question: If they are so bizarre and difficult to comprehend, how is physics able to study them?

The goal of science is to describe the laws of nature and their ramifications, that is, to arrive at a particular approximation of the laws that actually exist objectively and that are not contingent on our knowledge of them. But reality, nature, does not have to be similar to that with which we are familiar in our daily lives. Physics solves the problem by the use of symbols and describes the laws of nature using mathematical equations. Generally, we, human beings, do not understand these symbols, and we are unable to translate them into concepts with which we are familiar. However, to use a theory of physics, it is not necessary to understand its symbols, but it is crucial to know how to arrive at the experimental implications.

We can demonstrate the situation using a story that I told in my previous books. This is the story of Professor Feynman, one of the great physicists of the twentieth century:

> You can imagine to what lengths my father went in order to provide me a higher education. He sent me to study at MIT, I graduated from Princeton, returned home and my father says to me: "Now you have a good science education. I always aspired to understand something that I could never understand. My son, will you explain something to me?
>
> I answered, "Yes."
>
> He said, "I understand they say that light is given off by atoms when the atom passes from one state to another, from an excited state to a state of lower energy."
>
> I said, "That is correct."
>
> My father continued, "And light is a kind of particle, I think they call it a photon?"
>
> "Yes, that is correct."
>
> "Accordingly, if the photon is given off from the atom, while the atom is in its excited state, then the photon has to be inside the atom."

I responded, "Well, that is not so."

My father said, "So how can it be that a photon particle is given off by the atom and is not there?"

I thought for a few minutes, then answered: "I'm sorry; I don't know. I can't explain it to you."

He was very disappointed. All these years he tried to teach me something, and the result was so inadequate.

(*The Physics Teacher*, 1969, p. 319)

Here we have a clash of two ways of thinking. One is concrete, demanding an explanation in terms of day-to-day experience. The modern physicist, however, understands that reality is complex and cannot be perceived in terms of day-to-day experience. The physicist is already accustomed to symbolic language and is comfortable with his way of thinking. Feynman is not troubled by his father's question. He knows that the spontaneous emission of a photon can be described by the equations of quantum electrodynamics, and thus he has no need for a more concrete explanation. Moreover, the concrete "explanation" would not satisfy him at all.

Now, as we near the end of the section, let us think about what matter is, from a physical perspective. Let us consider the structure of matter, as described by modern physics. At room temperature, all matter exists in the form of liquids, gases or solid bodies. In all cases the matter is made up of atoms and molecules. Electrical and magnetic fields operate in between the atoms and molecules, and it is these that hold the matter in a solid, liquid or gaseous state. The molecules are made up of atoms, and the atoms themselves are made up of electrons and atomic nuclei, between which an electrical field operates. The atomic nuclei are made up of protons and neutrons which are held together by nuclear force.

Ultimately, all matter, even at extreme temperatures and pressures such as the matter in the sun, is comprised of elementary and sub-elementary particles (such as quarks and strings) and physical fields (electromagnetic, nuclear).

From a physical perspective all the volume of matter is taken up by physical fields, and the particles of matter do not take up any space at all. Sounds odd? We would expect that the particles of matter – electrons, protons, neutrons etc. – would take up, if not the majority of the volume of the matter, then at least a significant part of it. However, according to the principles of modern physics, the volume of all the particles in matter is equal to zero. Not a minuscule volume but absolutely zero volume! This does not mean that the particles do not exist and are not real. They are real and exist in dimensions smaller than three-dimensional space – they are points, or one-dimensional lines: strings. We have come to the conclusion that physical matter is a rather odd creature. It is composed of strange entities – physical fields which occupy all the volume of the matter and particles which do not occupy any volume whatsoever. This entity seems almost abstract, but nonetheless we shall continue to use the term matter, even though from a physical perspective, this use of the word is far from its original meaning. In the next section we will continue on our journey in the world of the laws of nature.

Let us pause for a moment and think about the idea of law and order in the world, the role of science being to explain it. We are used to the existence of lawfulness in nature, and just as we have become accustomed to other things and fail to see the wonder inherent in them, so we see nothing strange or surprising about the lawfulness of nature. If we are trying to understand the essence of things, then an absence of order and lawfulness would seem easier to understand. The absence of something needs no explanation, whereas the existence of the phenomenon generally does necessitate some elucidation. If you leave an empty notebook at home and come back to find that the pages are still empty, no explanation is needed. It is another story if you come home to find a passage of text written on one of the pages. Then we would need an explanation – where did the text come from?

This is an analogy. But what does it illustrate? The order in the inanimate world and the laws of nature that express that order are analogous to the text in the notebook. The order in nature and the laws of nature are not to be taken for granted. It is only our routine way of thinking that prevents us from appreciating the great wonder in the order of nature. The laws of nature formulated by mathematical equations are a comprehensive list of instructions that guide the physical entity in what it must do at every moment. Hence, every law of nature is a text, which contains a particular message. The existence of order in the world requires an explanation. From a godless worldview this is a great mystery. One can say that the laws of nature, and their reflection, the laws of science, are a creation – more than that – a sublime, exquisite creation. And again the question arises: Who created it? From a secular perspective there is no answer to this question – it is a mystery, but no true inquiring scientist can ignore this question. Thus wrote Albert Einstein:

Certain it is that a conviction, akin to religious feeling, of the rationality or intelligibility of the world lies behind all scientific work of higher order.

This firm belief, a belief bound up with deep feeling, in a superior mind that reveals itself in the world of experience, represents my conception of God. (*Ideas and Opinions*, p. 202)

A long time ago, philosophers discovered the wonder inherent in our world. At the beginning of the chapter I brought the words of the psalmist: "How great are Your works, O Lord, You have made them all with wisdom; the earth is full of Your possessions." (Psalms 104:24). In a discussion about belief in the creator of the world the philosopher Francis Bacon (1561-1626) wrote: "Certainely a little Philosophie inclineth mans minde to Atheisme, but depth in Philosophie bringeth men about to Religion."[3] (We must remember that at that time the word 'philosophy' was synonymous with knowledge of the world.) And David Hume (1711-1776) explained this as follows: People are fed all kinds of preconceptions, which reinforce their beliefs. But when "they discover... that the course of nature is regular and uniform, their whole faith totters, and falls to ruin. But being taught, by more reflection, that this very regularity and uniformity is the strongest proof of design and of a supreme intelligence, they return to that belief, which they had deserted; and they are now able to establish it on a firmer and more durable foundation."[4]

And here is another testimony from Einstein of a supreme intelligence that he discovers as a result of scientific elucidation:

[The scientist's] religious feeling takes the form of a rapturous amazement at the harmony of natural law, which reveals an intelligence of such superiority that, compared with it, all the systematic thinking and acting of human beings becomes an utterly insignificant reflection.[5]

It should be emphasized that the statement that there is lawfulness in nature is not a scientific claim, and nor does it derive from any scientific laws. From a secular perspective, one that is devoid of God, there can be no rational argument

---

3. *The works of Fr. Bacon, Vol. VII.* London, 1826, p. 48
4. *The Natural History of Religion*, p. 51
5. *Ideas and Opinions*, p. 40

for the existence of laws in the world. Einstein writes: "the success of such a project presupposes a high degree of ordering of the objective world, and this could not be expected a priori. That is the 'miracle' which is being constantly reinforced as our knowledge expands."[6] Scientific development brings new evidence for the existence of the surprising order in the world of nature. *This is the "wonder", the "gap" in the secular view. It is a "gap" that does not disappear with the development of science, but is "being constantly reinforced". From the point of view of the believer, the order in the world indicates the existence of its creator.*

2. The Spiritual World

"'Heaven' and 'earth' symbolize... matter and spirit of which the world is composed. This means that at the start of creation God created the two principal components of our world: 'heaven' – spirit, and 'earth' – matter."

(Rabbi Joseph Dov Halevi Soloveitchik, *Man and His World*, p. 231)

Great intellectual effort is required to grasp the concept of a *spiritual world*. In general, comprehending the existence and substance of spiritual entities is extremely difficult for a person who is not used to thinking about abstract things. Physical reality is so self-evident, that it is hard to imagine that there could be entities in the world that are not physical. We saw above that the thing that is closest to us – the soul of each and every one of us – is not physical, but spiritual. Likewise the source of all reality, which gives meaning to our existence in this world – God – is the ultimate, all-encompassing spiritual entity. But the world is also full of another kind of spiritual entity, the presence of which we became accustomed to a long time ago.

---

6. *Letters to Solovine*: 30.III.52

Let us look at a particular text, such as an essay or a story. This text is printed on paper, using a certain font, ink and language. However, it can also be translated into another language and printed using a different font. One could use different ink or another kind of paper, and nowadays we can even dispense with the need for paper and ink, and just keep the text in electronic form, such as in our computer's memory. So, the question is, what remains fixed here? What does not change with all these transformations? The answer is clear: the content of the text, which is not dependent on physical means, does not change. We must distinguish, therefore, between the spiritual message of the text and the material means of delivering it – between the message and the medium.

The content of the text is the spiritual essence, and the role of the physical medium is only to safeguard it. But when it comes to the life of human beings a spiritual message will never appear without a physical shell. Hence, one might get the impression that it is a necessary thing – the spiritual entity must be accompanied by the matter that safeguards it. It is extremely difficult, if not impossible, to imagine pure spiritual entities which are not embodied by matter.

Nonetheless, an analysis of the structure of science reveals a spiritual entity which is not dependent on physical means – the laws of nature. The aim of physics is to reveal, formulate and describe the laws of nature and to investigate their implications. As we have said, the physicist describes the laws of nature in the language of mathematics, using mathematical equations. The content of these equations is a kind of collection of instructions that show what a physical system must do at every moment and how it must develop. Two examples of this are Maxwell's equations which describe the electromagnetic field and Einstein's equations that describe the gravitational fields.

$$\text{div}\mathbf{E} = 4\pi\sigma$$

$$\text{rot}\mathbf{E} + \frac{1}{c}\frac{\partial \mathbf{H}}{\partial t} = 0$$

$$\text{div}\mathbf{H} = 0$$

$$\text{rot}\mathbf{H} - \frac{1}{c}\frac{\partial \mathbf{E}}{\partial t} = \frac{4\pi}{c}.$$

$$R_{\mu v} - \tfrac{1}{2}Rg_{\mu v} + \Lambda g_{\mu v} = -\kappa T_{\mu v}$$

One does not need to be an expert in theoretical physics or understand what these equations mean to comprehend that these are texts with a particular content and message. In other words, these are spiritual entities. It would seem that these entities are no different from those that we discussed above, they are embodied in the matter of print media or other media that are required to preserve their content. However, a deeper look reveals "pure" spiritual entities, which are not embodied in matter.

We have already stated that the laws of physics, and the mathematical equations that express them, are an approximation to the laws of nature. In fact, they are kinds of reflections of the laws of nature that are correct to a particular approximation and are discovered and formulated by human beings. However, modern physics is only a few centuries old and prior to that people did not think about the existence of equations that express the laws of nature at all. In fact, if we look at the history of the world, we see that there was a fairly long period of time during which human beings did not exist at all, while the laws of nature did exist. Nature has developed, and continues to develop all the time, in accordance with these laws. In other words, the laws of nature are a spiritual entity, one which has not been written down using any physical medium. It is hard, if not impossible, for us to imagine the existence of a pure spiritual entity which is not embodied in any matter whatsoever.

The laws of nature are a file of precise instructions which determine the development of nature at any moment. Here the question arises: How does a spiritual entity which contains particular instructions operate those instructions on nature? Is it even possible? This is a global question but in order to answer it, it is best to go down to the human level, the level which is more familiar to us. In Chapter One, which discusses the wonder of man, we saw that each and every person has the amazing ability to connect with the spiritual world of human culture, and thereby to introduce into his own memory a part of humankind's collective memory. Karl Popper, an eminent thinker in the field of philosophy of science, describes the situation in the following way. Our world contains three worlds: the world of matter, the physical world – world one; the world of our souls – world 2; and the world of human knowledge – world three. Clearly Popper's world three does not contain the entire spiritual world. For example, the laws of nature that have not yet been discovered are not part of the world of human knowledge that exists at this time. We can say that Popper's world three is the accessible spiritual world, which is part of the entire spiritual world. We will talk more about what this means in due course.

For example, a particular physical theory includes the basis for building both a nuclear reactor and a nuclear bomb. This theory exists in the accessible spiritual world and is documented using items in the material world – books, articles, computer software and the memories of scientists. The theory, which is a spiritual entity, is incapable, on its own, of creating any positive benefit or causing any damage. In the absence of a connection between the spiritual entity – the physical theory in the spiritual world – and the world of matter, matter cannot be affected by it. A scientific theory can have an effect on matter only when a person "mediates" between the theory and the world of matter, and acts to bring it to fruition. The person, the scientist or engineer, studies the physical theory, the plans and the engineering documents and builds a nuclear reactor, operates it and *supervises its operation*.

Man affects matter using all kinds of movements of his limbs, which are also part of the material world, but ultimately it is the person's soul that operates the connection between the spiritual, scientific entity and the matter. We come across countless examples of this in our everyday lives. Human beings utilize stores of knowledge and produce tools, machines, cars, computers etc. After a particular device or machine is made, it is the person who *operates* and *supervises* it. The person operates the car and drives it, and even though the functioning of the car is assured by the precise execution of its design, continuous *supervision* of its operation is crucial – one must hold on to the steering wheel so as not to veer off the road and one must control the speed by accelerating and braking. Without this *supervision,* an accident is inevitable. The same applies to man's control over his body. Once a person decides how he is going to behave, he has to constantly supervise his body and its movements. Here we come to the three-part model: man's mind creates a link between the spiritual entity and the physical entity, and monitors its continued existence. In other words, the mind uses a particular spiritual entity as an operating system for a particular physical entity. The mind can take this spiritual entity from the spiritual world (in particular from the accessible spiritual world – world three), or from a built-in spiritual world within man. We all have a complex and sophisticated spiritual system, the nervous system, including the brain itself. We call it a *spiritual system* because the nervous system is primarily a spiritual entity, and its content is expressed using the physical means of a person's limbs. In relatively simple actions, such as walking, moving the hands and the like, the mind uses the complex and sophisticated operating system that exists within man.

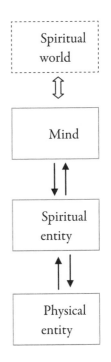

In more complex actions, such as the building of different machines, the mind also uses the content and the theories of the spiritual world that is external to man. This connection is illustrated at the top of the diagram above.

I believe that the three-part model also describes the nature of divine creation and providence. I should point out here that I am not *anthropomorphizing* God's actions; rather I am *deifying* the actions of man. Man *was created in the image of God*, and studying man's behavior and actions described above can give us a hint about the nature of divine providence and may lead us to a deeper understanding of it. God created a world comprised of a spiritual world and a physical world, and He creates a connection between them. The laws of nature are a part of the divine spiritual world and God operates them and imposes them on matter. This sentence requires some clarification. The movement of lumps of matter, just like the movement of Earth or other planets around the sun, complies with the laws of physics. The existence of any physical object, of a ballistic missile or the most minute particle of matter, is dependent on the operation of the laws of nature on them. Their existence is conditional on the spiritual world which operates on them.

Here we must be precise. It is not accurate to think that without the *presence* of a spiritual entity such as the laws of physics matter cannot not exist. It would be correct to say that *without the imposition of the laws of physics on matter, matter cannot exist.* Without God *imposing* the spiritual entity – the laws of nature – on nature, nature does not exist. This is what is meant by the claim that the world is *contingent* – at every moment the matter in the world is contingent on God who imposes the spiritual world on it. This spiritual world is God's operating system, but it is not sufficient for it simply to be *present*. If it is not operated, the material world does not exist, and it is God who does this. Similarly, it is not enough that a particular physical theory exists in the accessible spiritual world (world three) for it to have an effect on matter (world one). A physical theory can only affect the world of matter when man uses that theory.

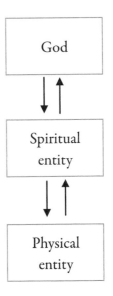

The diagram below represents the way in which the divine spiritual world controls the material world. One might say that it is the constant providence that operates the world. In the example above, a person produces the car, operates it and supervises its actions. An outside observer of the movement of the car traveling at a fixed speed on a straight road might think that it moves solely according to the laws of physics, but the truth is that the driver is in control of the car's movements at every moment. In the same way, we also mistakenly think that the world develops solely according to the laws of nature, without God's supervision, whereas in fact divine supervision is constantly acting, and the laws of nature are simply tools for His providence.

In the two models above the parallel is drawn between man's soul and God. This parallel has a strong basis in our tradition. In the Babylonian Talmud, it tells of five similarities between man's soul and body and the power of God in the world.

> Just as the Holy One, blessed be He, fills the whole world, so the soul fills the whole body. Just as the Holy One, blessed be He, sees but is not seen, so the soul sees but is not seen. Just as the Holy One, blessed be He, sustains the whole world, so the soul sustains the whole body. Just as the Holy One, blessed be He, is pure, so the soul is pure. Just as the Holy One, blessed be He, sits in the innermost chambers, so the soul dwells in the innermost chambers.[7]

---

7. *Brachot*, 10a

One might say that the supervision and the involvement of the spirit in the actions of matter do not contradict the laws of physics; they operate in addition to them. But we will discuss this more later on.

In the discussion above we spoke about the laws of nature as one part of the overall spiritual world. According to the Jewish view, the spiritual and material world together are a divine creation which develops over the course of time: "In the beginning God created the heaven and the earth", the word "heaven" symbolizing the spiritual world and "earth" the material world. Professor Yehuda Levi mentions in his book, *Torah and Science*, (p. 161) that the Hebrew word "*shamayim*" (heaven) sometimes refers to spiritual worlds only (like the word *heaven* in English). And according to Nachmanides, (in his commentary on the Bible, Genesis 1:9), the word *shamayim* in the first verse of Genesis refers to spiritual values only, and does not include the spheres, the heavenly bodies, i.e. the sun, moon and stars; all of these are included in the word "*eretz*" (land).

Of course the divine spiritual world is rich and diverse, and the laws of nature are only a part of it. According to the Jewish view, which is based on the Bible, God is the creator of the world, of its laws and its order, and He supervises it. God created a world that is comprised of two parts, or two worlds – a spiritual world and a physical world. In fact, the vast majority of the Bible is dedicated to a discussion of the spiritual world.

The word "*spirit*" is defined by the dictionary as: "an abstract realm, a realm of the intellect and ethics", while the concept of "*spiritual*" is defined as: "belonging to the abstract realm or to the realm of the intellect and ethics, theoretical, belonging to the spirit (the opposite of material, physical)".

The concept of a spiritual entity is very deeply rooted in the Jewish tradition. Rabbi Yehuda Halevi, in the *Kuzari*, refers to the "Book of Creation": "The Book is constructed on the mystery of ten units ...: 'Ten Sefiroth without anything else; close thy mouth from speaking, close thy heart from thinking..."" (Part Four, 27). Rabbi Shlomo Aviner explains: "The expression '*b'lima*' [without anything else] means 'without essence'. Namely, there is no physical thing here that can be felt. Human small-mindedness has led man to think that only that which can be felt is reality, is real, whereas the holy, the spiritual, the exalted have no substance, they are not reality. But the opposite is true: the more abstract something is, the more '*b'lima*', the stronger than reality, the more substantial." (*Commentary on the Kuzari*, Part Four, pages 269-270). Maimonides says about those who do not believe in spiritual reality: "That which is not body, nor a bodily event [anything related to the body or descriptions of it, such as strength and weakness, meanness and kindness etc.] cannot be found amongst the foolish... it was clear to [wise people] that everything that is distinct from matter has a stronger reality than material things. In fact it is not correct to say 'stronger', rather that the distinct reality is more real – since no change can affect it [as all objects are constantly changing, and their existence is temporary. But the spiritual that is distinct from the physical – that is permanent and eternal]. (*Treatise on the Resurrection of the Dead*, 353) And Rabbi Moshe Chaim Luzzato, in his book *Derech Hashem* (*The Way of God*), writes: "Creation in general consists of two basic parts: the physical and the spiritual. The physical is that which we experience with our senses...and the spiritual consists of all entities which are not physical, which cannot be detected by physical means..." (Part One, beginning of Chapter 5).

Rabbi Eliyahu Dessler connects spirituality with the laws of nature and with the essence of nature:

> The plan and purpose of creation is its spiritual content. Everything that exists in the physical world has a spiritual source. Its development, its activity, how it affects other things and is affected by them—all these take place according to spiritual needs, and to serve the spiritual ends set by the Creator for His creation. This is how

our Rabbis interpret the verse "If not for My covenant day and night, I had not established the laws of heaven and earth..." Even the laws of nature depend on the spiritual purpose contained in the covenant of the Torah. What appears to us as a self-contained system of natural laws is only an illusion. Many sayings of our Sages illustrate this principle; above all the twice-repeated statement in the morning blessings for light: "He who renews each day continually the works of creation." By this they teach us that we are not to consider the principle creation as something created once at a point of time in the past and since then existing by its own power, but as something that needs to be "re-created" each day and each moment–"continually." (*Letter from Eliyahu*–Published in English as *Strive for Truth*, 252)

However, the physical and the spiritual world are not of equal standing. The existence of the physical world is dependent, every moment, on the spiritual world: "The root of its existence is in spirituality", and modern physics reinforces this. In the previous chapter we came to the conclusion that physical matter is a rather strange thing. It is composed of different entities – physical fields which occupy all the volume of the matter and particles that do not occupy any volume at all. The physical field is somewhat similar to a spiritual object – at every point in space it exists in potential, as a possibility. Only when a charge is placed at a particular point in the space does the force act on it. What characterizes the field is the *information*, about what is supposed to happen at every point in the space when a charge is placed there. In a sense, the physical field is a field of information, but it is clear that this information is a spiritual entity without which the field does not exist. Another component of matter is quantum particles. We can show that here too the spiritual essence is the determining factor, and we have stated that the existence of a spiritual essence is necessary for the existence of matter, but it is not sufficient – without God operating it, matter does not exist at all. In this context, I would like to bring up a topic that emerges somewhat surprisingly here, and that is:

Science and Kabbalah (Jewish mysticism)

If we look at the Bible, we see that even though it tells us a lot about God's revelations and His connection with the prophets, the Bible does not tell us a thing about God Himself. Acquiring an understanding of what God is, even if it is only a partial understanding, is a task undertaken by the Kabbalah. It should be emphasized that the task taken on by the Kabbalah to reveal the hidden essence behind the external forms in reality is no less important today than ever before. "For as long as nature and man are conceived as His creations, and that is the indispensable condition of highly developed religious life, the quest for the hidden life of the transcendent element in such creation will always form one of the most important preoccupations of the human mind."[8]

A few words about the content of the Kabbalah and its tools. As stated above, the goal of the Kabbalah is to penetrate, as far as possible, into the spiritual world of God, while it is clear that man does not possess appropriate concepts with which to describe it, even to give a partial description. We draw our concepts from our experience, and in the field of the divine we have no experience. Hence, philosophy, which has created concepts of this kind and uses them, is not capable of dealing with this area. Analogies are commonly used in philosophical thought, but neither the analogy nor its interpretation can break through to an area that is beyond our comprehension. What is the conceptual breakthrough of the Kabbalah? Philosophers created concepts while the Kabbalists created symbols. Symbols are the main tool for describing a reality which in itself, and according to its own laws, has no expression in our world of

---

8.   Gershom Scholem, Major Trends in Jewish Mysticism, p. 38

concepts. Clearly a symbol cannot be translated into any language. Every symbol is a new word that is not derived from any existing concept, and every true symbol has an element of secrecy. Our goal here is not to enter into a description of specific Kabbalistic symbols, but it is important to stress what the goal of the language of symbols is, and what it is supposed to describe.

At this point I should remind you that the subject of this chapter is the divine spiritual world, and that is also the subject of the Kabbalah. We have seen that the spiritual world is like God's operating system. Nature functions by the operation of the laws of nature on matter, with God operating them, just as man's soul operates his nervous system. The Kabbalah describes the spiritual world through the system of spheres. We do not need to enter into a detailed description of the spheres in order to see that they are an attempt to comprehend different aspects of the divine spiritual world. Gershom Scholem describes the Kabbalah thus: "The Kabbalist who yearns for the life-flow concealed in all things, finds it also in the divine itself. The unity of God is the unity of his concealed life, with the life of man and the lives of all the worlds attached to them. The flow of this life and its fixed pace – is what appears in the "spheres" which all Kabbalist literature expounds on, using the language of allusion and symbol. The spheres are waves of the concealed life of the divine, which emanate from the infinite depths to the creation, and the greatness of this abundance is the hidden and mysterious internality of the creation itself." (Dvarim be-go, p. 250) [My translation]

Now let us return to our subject – the laws of nature as a component of the divine spiritual world. It is important to stress again that the laws of nature are one of the tools of providence. The overflow that comes from the supreme source reaches nature and the soul of man. In Judaism in general, and in the Kabbalistic tradition in particular, the soul is seen as a spark of the divine source, and as such it has an inseparable connection with its course. But let us return to the laws of nature – as one of the conduits of providence and as a part of the spiritual world. Here a surprise awaits us: in a sense, the objectives of modern science are identical to those of the Kabbalah!

Let us think for a moment not about science in general but specifically about physics. One can distinguish two aspects of physics – the applied and the cognitive. Everyone is familiar with the incredible achievements of physics in the applied, technological realm. From time immemorial human beings have been interested in finding out about the world in which they live. Science in general and particularly physics provide an answer, to a certain extent, to these desires. We have seen that the laws of nature, and the laws of physics that reflect them, are part of the divine spiritual world, the spiritual world being God's system for operating the world. Looking at it from this perspective, the purpose of physics is to understand this divine system. Similarly, the goal of the theoretical Kabbalah is to understand the divine system that operates nature and man. Hence theoretical physics fulfills the objective of the Kabbalah that is related to understanding the way in which nature works.

The tools that physics uses to understand the spiritual world are also similar to those used by the Kabbalah – physics describes the world using symbols. The language of symbols used by physics is the language of mathematics. It is necessary to use symbols because there are no human symbols that would be able to describe the divine spiritual world. The great scientists were aware to a certain extent that the goal of their research is to understand the divine operating system. Isaac Newton likened infinite space to God's sensory system ("sensorium") – incorporeal, living, intelligent, omnipresent, which sees all things intimately and connects with us through our little sensoriums, and thus understands our thoughts.[9] Newton writes: "The omnipresent God is acknowledged and

---

9. Optics, Query p. 28

by the Jews is called Place."[10] Albert Einstein thought that one cannot be a truly great scientist without a religious feeling, and we have already quoted him above: "[The scientist's] religious feeling takes the form of rapturous amazement at the harmony of a natural law, which reveals an intelligence of such superiority that, compared with it, all the systematic thinking and acting of human beings becomes an utterly insignificant reflection."[11] A secular thinker, Karl Popper, expresses a similar view: "It is his intuition, his mystical insight into the nature of things, rather than his reasoning, which makes a great scientist... Creativeness is an entirely irrational, a mystical faculty..."[12]

The connection, or similarity, between science and the Kabbalah may seem strange or artificial. But it would appear from the arguments that I brought above that the two have common objectives in the realm of the divine, and that the two approach these objectives in a similar way – using symbols.

We will continue our discussion on secularism in the conclusion of the next section, which is a continuation of the study of the divine spiritual world.

3. The Unity of the World and the Laws of Nature

The prohibition against making idols and images attests to a very important principle in Judaism. The second of the Ten Commandments declares: "You shall not make for yourself a graven image or any likeness which is in the heavens above, which is on the earth below, or which is in the water beneath the earth" (Exodus 20:4). The unity of God, when it is contrasted with the multitude of gods of mythology, necessitated

---

10. Westfall, R.S., *Never at Rest*, p. 511

11. *Ideas and Opinions*, p. 40

12. *The Open Society and Its Enemies,* volume II, Hegel and Marx, p.228. The emphasis here, and in all the quotations throughout the book, are mine. B.F.

God's lack of visual appearance. This was one of the most revolutionary steps in the history of humankind. According to pagan belief, the gods exist everywhere and they are different from one place to the next. This is how the servants of the King of Aram explained that the God of the Jews lives in the mountains: "And the servants of the king of Aram said unto him: 'Their God is a God of the hills; therefore they were stronger than we; but let us fight against them in the plain, and surely we shall be stronger than they'" (Kings I 20:23).

Despite the conceptual and ideological revolution that began with the revelation at Mount Sinai, the pagan view has not yet disappeared from human culture, and it has survived in the modern world as materialist philosophy. This philosophy was born in pagan Greece and it represents a modern form of nature worship. According to this view, the source of everything, including spirituality is materia. This is in contrast with the message that we received at Mount Sinai that God is the ultimate spiritual entity, the source of both materiality and spirituality. Judaism imposes an absolute prohibition on naturalism – the pure naturalist ideology. Anyone who claims that he believes in God must rid himself of any hint of materiality in his reference to God. Judaism has always struggled with the pagan approach, which worships material objects, and Maimonides even devoted a substantial part of his Guide of the Perplexed to the struggle with attributing physical descriptions to God.

There is not a hint of truth in the claim that the materialist approach is supported by the achievements of science. We have already spoken about this, and I am again emphasizing the weakness of the widely held view of a world that has always developed of its own accord and which is even capable of giving meaning to our lives. This is nothing but paganism at its very best. As we have stated, one of the aims of this book is to uproot from the very core the preconception that the world and its development can be explained scientifically and without God.

One of the most prominent and important characteristics of modern science is the principle of the uniformity of the laws of nature, that is, that the laws of nature are the same everywhere in the world. Nowadays scientists accept this as self-evident, but the routine of our lives and our thinking prevents us from discerning the wonders of the world and its amazing qualities. The concept of the uniformity of the laws of nature has become part of our mentality, but this was not always the case. Conceptually, this was a new idea which Isaac Newton assimilated into the metaphysical infrastructure of modern science. Prior to Newton, the accepted wisdom was that the heavenly bodies, just like all other bodies, have their own laws. Newton's belief in the unity of the world and the uniformity of its laws derived from his religious worldview, which was closely connected to Jewish thought. It would not be far-fetched to suggest that there may be a causal connection between the inception of modern science in Christian Europe and the element of Jewish thought in Judeo-Christian civilization.[13]

We can ask ourselves why the laws of physics, or the laws of nature in general, are the same everywhere in the universe. The assertion of the universality, the generality and the uniformity of the laws of nature in time and space cannot be explained by science, that is, scientifically. And the reason for this is simple: the assertion of the uniformity of the laws of nature relates to the nature of the laws – which laws should be in the world. The answer to this question must be outside of science, outside of the laws of nature. Super-scientific, supernatural considerations are needed to answer this question. But when we abandon the belief that nature is everything that exists in the world, the issue of the uniformity of the laws of nature seems extremely odd. Thus Vitaly Ginzburg, one of the distinguished physicists of our time, and a teacher of mine at the beginning of my scientific career, writes: "My atheist view is the intuitive

13. Burtt E.A.: The Metaphysical Foundations of Modern Science; Whitehead A. N.: Science and the Modern World

claim that there is nothing but nature and the laws that govern it." From the atheist's point of view, nature is the ultimate, final, absolute reality and the laws of nature are an inseparable part of it. The laws of nature are an inherent part of nature; they are contained within it – they are immanent. Many atheist thinkers hold this view, according to which the laws of nature are actually part of nature. Now let us think about different places in the world. When we adopt this view that the law is a derivative of nature, there is no necessity for the same laws to exist in different locations. If nature "produces" its laws, then we are entirely justified in asking the question as to how nature in one place can "know" which laws it applies in another place which is light years from the first. The identity of the laws in different locations is a mystery, a riddle that cannot be explained according to the view of the immanent law. Karl Popper expresses it thus: "The structural homogeneity of the world seems to resist any 'deeper' explanation: it remains a mystery."[14]

On the other hand, there is no mystery in the fact that the laws are the same all over the universe when the source of the law is *external* and above nature, when the law is a command of God. Such a command is not related to one place or another, it is above nature. In our view, the laws of nature are part of the divine spiritual world, and the question about the connection between them and the location in the universe does not even arise. The laws of nature belong to the spiritual world, and *consequently they are not dependent on location, or in other words: they are identical in every place in the world*. So, within Jewish thought there is a solution to a problem to which there is no solution in naturalist, pagan thought of the deification of nature, or, to be more precise, the idolization of nature.

Now we can continue with our discussion on the inadequacy of the secular approach in describing the world. In the last two sections we discussed the spiritual aspect of our

---

14. K. Popper, *Realism and the Aim of Science*, p. 152

world – the spiritual world. This is the point where the two worldviews – the Jewish-religious worldview and the secular, godless worldview – diverge. The secular worldview is not uniform: at one extreme is the ultimate materialist approach which identifies the spirituality of human beings with movements of matter, while at the other extreme is the approach which sees man's spirituality as a spiritual entity. However, what all of these secular approaches have in common is the negation of the spirit as an entity that is independent of man – a negation of the existence of the spirit outside of man and humankind.

In the previous section I presented the three worlds of Karl Popper. In a sense this is the highest level of understanding our world that it is possible to achieve using secular rational tools. Popper recognizes the objectivity of the spiritual world of human culture, world three in his terminology. But this world, according to Popper, is all the result of man. All items in this world, such as various scientific theories, are inventions of human beings; that is to say, without humankind a spiritual world would not exist. And not only is the source of world three in humankind, its objectivity is also contingent on the presence of human beings. One can try to imagine (luckily we only have to imagine it!) that the majority of human culture was destroyed: all the stores of information – books, manuscripts, computer software and the like – destroyed. But that is not enough – we have a large amount of knowledge in our own minds. I personally would be able to reconstruct from my memory classical mechanics, the law of gravity, the theory of the electromagnetic field, quantum theory and the theory of special and general relativity. Therefore, let us try to imagine that human memory has also been erased. Should all of this happen, humankind would return to the state it was in thousands of years ago!

According to Popper, scientific theory and the laws of physics are an invention of man, and their appearance in world three is dated at the time of publication of the theory. But what was there prior to the creation of the theories by Newton or Einstein? Did the laws of nature, the laws of physics, exist? There is no doubt that the wording of any particular law of nature is dependent on human beings, but the law itself and its scientific implications have an objective existence which is not dependent on any person. Every person speaks his own language, but the content of his words is not dependent on one language or another.

It is interesting to compare the idea of the reality of world three with that of the spiritual world in general. According to Popper, the reality of world three is derived from the fact that items in it, such as scientific theories, are able to affect the physical world, world one. But this effect is contingent on the mediation of a human being. In other words, whenever man is not mediating between world three and world one – he is not using world three items to affect world one – world three has no reality. Without man, without humanity, world three is "dead". To put it another way, man is the source of the reality of world three. This is not the case from the point of view of Jewish thought. God is the source of the reality of all things. The spiritual world was created by God, and it is God who imposes it on the material world. God is the source of the reality of both the physical and the spiritual worlds and the reality of world three, the reality of human culture, is derived from the reality of the spiritual world in general.

Here we can see clearly the "gap" in the secular approach: the laws of nature, which, realistically, must be the perpetual cause of the world and its development, even before the appearance of man on this earth, are linked to humankind, which is in fact the source of their reality! This is the direct result of the denial of a spiritual entity outside of man. How, then, does the secular philosopher respond to the question about the existence of the laws of nature prior to the appearance of man? Immanuel Kant, the preeminent advocate of the secular approach, came to the conclusion that it is man who determines the laws of nature and imposes them on nature! Later on, in the chapters on understanding the world, we will see the unreasonableness of this extreme position, even though it is the logical consequence of secular principles such as the denial of the existence of a creator who intervenes in the matters of the world and the replacement of God with man.

In this chapter we have also come across another "gap" in the secular worldview – its inability to explain the uniformity of the laws of nature everywhere in the world, even in places millions and billions of light years from one another. Earlier we quoted Karl Popper: "The structural homogeneity of the world seems to resist any 'deeper' explanation: it remains a mystery." Popper was, of course, aware of Kant's "ingenious" solution, "that our intellect does not read the laws in nature's open book, but imposes its own laws upon nature."[15] But despite his adherence to these ideas, it seems that Popper's realistic approach was not compatible with Kant's arguments. Popper's adherence to the secular approach that denies any source of spirituality outside of man brought him to a dead end in his attempt to comprehend the uniformity of the laws of nature. One way or another, the uniformity of the laws of nature constitutes a "gap" in the fabric of secular thought.

---

15. Ibid, p.152

4. A "Scientific" World Governed Solely by the Laws of Nature

In the first chapter we mentioned the determinism of classical physics and the non-determinism of quantum physics, and we will talk more about that later. One can say that the major point of contention between the Jewish approach and the approach that deifies nature is in the question of determinism or non-determinism in the world. The will of God and man's free will are not compatible with a deterministic world, a world in which everything is predetermined from the first moment of creation, a world in which God Himself is subject to the necessity of causality. Hence it is important that we understand this concept – determinism – a little better.

Intuitively, one can summarize the concept of determinism by comparing the world to a film at the cinema. The picture that we are seeing right now in the film represents the present, the parts of the film that have already been screened represent the past, and all the parts of the film that have not yet been screened represent the future. In a film, the future exists together with the past; it is firmly fixed in the same way as the past is firmly fixed. Its existence is as real as the existence of the past. The viewer may not know the events in the future, but in principle all the future events, without exception, can be known with absolute certainty exactly like the events in the past. In fact, the future is known in full detail by the film's producer – the creator of the world. As a matter of fact the origin of the concept of determinism is religious, though not from Judaism. Religious determinism is connected to the concept of divine omnipotence – God's absolute control over the future – and divine omniscience, namely that the future is known by God now, and hence it is known and determined in advance. From a secular perspective, the determinism of the world is connected to the action of the laws of nature, on the premise that they describe all that is in the world, including human beings.

I do not accept this premise. We saw above that there are numerous unique phenomena, which are not governed by the laws of nature. The most important thing, which we will talk about in the next chapter, is that the premise that the laws of nature control everything in the world contradicts the existence of free will and divine providence. However, it is impossible to logically prove the incorrectness of premises of this kind, since these are metaphysical truths which cannot be proved or refuted either by logic or by experience, and they are actually beliefs. However, we can test them by their consequences. Hence, let us temporarily adopt, for the purpose of the discussion, the premise that everything in the world is governed solely by the laws of nature.

Let us examine two possibilities – one is that the laws of nature are deterministic (like classical physics), and the second is that the laws of nature are non-deterministic (like quantum physics). In the first chapter we saw that macroscopic bodies, such as objects that we see all around us, as well as the heavenly bodies, generally move and develop according to deterministic laws, while tiny particles (such as atoms, molecules and electrons), from which all objects are made, obey the non-deterministic quantum laws.

Let us start with the deterministic laws of nature. We are, of course, aware of the fact that the deterministic laws are only an approximation to the real laws of nature. But, to a degree, we are able to use this approximation to describe the development of macroscopic bodies over time. Even though I, like most scientists, wholeheartedly believe that the real laws of nature are non-deterministic, there have been scientists, amongst them Albert Einstein, who believed in the deterministic nature of the laws of nature. Either way, we will now study a world that is directed by deterministic laws of nature.

What does it mean that a particular system is directed by deterministic laws? This means that the position of the system at a particular time unequivocally determines everything that will happen to it, namely its position at every other time. For example, according to the principles of classical physics, if we know at a particular point in time the locations and speeds of all the particles in a particular system, and the physical fields that are acting upon them, then we can predict everything that will happen to that system, and reconstruct everything that has happened.

According to these principles, if we know all the physical details of the world at the moment of creation, it is possible to know and to predict everything that will happen in the world at all points in time. In other words, everything that happens in the world now and everything that will happen in the future is determined unequivocally at the moment of the creation of the world. According to this, all the great creative works of human culture were also determined at the first moment of creation. And everything that I am doing and also everything that you, the reader, are doing right now, and everything that I will do tomorrow and at any other time in the future, was all determined at the start of creation. As Nobel Prize winner John Eccles remarks in The Self and Its Brain:

I would like to add a comment about determinism. If physical determinism is true, then that is the end of all discussion or argument; everything is finished. There is no philosophy. All human persons are caught up in this inexorable web of circumstances and cannot break out of it. Everything that we think we are doing is an illusion and that is that. Will anybody live up to this situation? It even comes to this, that the laws of physics and all our understanding of physics is the result of the same inexorable web of circumstances. It isn't a matter any more of our struggling for truth to understand what this natural world is and how it came to be and what are the springs of its operation. All of this is illusion. If we want to have that purely deterministic physical world, then we should remain silent.[16]

---

16. *The Self and Its Brain*, p. 546

In short, a deterministic world is a world of robots, whose movements are all pre-determined. They have no independent free will and hence there is no value in their actions or behavior. In fact, the very concept of "value" has no meaning. Nor does the concept of "meaning" have any meaning. This is a world of the utterly absurd. There were philosophers in Ancient Greece, Aristotle in particular, who believed in the existence of a transcendent God, but they did permit him one role – that of being "the first mover", who set the world in motion at the time of creation, and since that time He does not intervene in the matters of the world, but leaves it to the laws of nature to manage the world exclusively. It is clear that there is no significant difference between this kind of belief and atheism.

Now let us imagine a world that is directed by non-deterministic laws of nature, like those of quantum theory. We have seen that tiny particles – atoms, molecules, electrons etc – from which all macroscopic objects are built, obey non-deterministic laws. In the first chapter we saw that the quantum laws do not unequivocally determine what will happen in a quantum system in the future, even if we have the maximum information about its position at a particular point in time. Quantum theory gives us only likelihoods, possibilities, chances. For example, if an atom is in an excited state, it may emit light, or to be more precise, a photon, the smallest unit of light. Quantum theory is able to predict that sooner or later the atom will emit a photon, but it is not able to predict when this will happen. Quantum theory is only able to provide a distribution of probabilities that the atom will emit a photon at one time or another. But when we are talking about a single atom, probabilities do not help. Only in a large group of atoms can the predictions of quantum theory be tested. To put it another way, between the cause – an atom in an excited state – and the effect – the emission of a photon – there is a loose, indefinite connection. The photon will be emitted but there is no law that determines at what point that will occur. The predictions of quantum theory are not unequivocal, and in the case described above there is no way to determine when the effect of the cause will come. Thus the laws of quantum theory do not explicitly and unequivocally determine the future.

Even though the macroscopic objects are generally governed (at a good approximation) by the deterministic laws of classical physics, there may be situations in which movements of quantum particles, of which macroscopic objects are comprised, affect the movements of these objects. Later we will bring examples of this, but in any event, a world in which the fundamental laws are non-deterministic and do not unequivocally determine the future is itself a non-deterministic world, whose future is not pre-determined. Now let us go back to the film analogy. If we were to record the entire process of development of the world on film, then every replay would show a completely different development, each replay would be a new film.

Now how is a world managed by non-deterministic laws different from one managed by deterministic laws which unequivocally determine the future? In both cases the laws of nature (and the initial conditions) are the exclusive cause that determine the development of the world. In the case of the classic deterministic laws, there is, in principle, a possibility of predicting the development of the world in advance. In contrast, in the case of the quantum laws it is impossible to predict the development of the world, even if we have the maximum information about its position at a particular point in time, such as at the time of creation. The difference is in the realm of the information, not in the nature of the development of the world. In such a world, as in a world managed by deterministic laws, there is no room for man's free will and God's involvement, as it is not they, but the laws of nature, that determine everything.

Let us consider further the concept of determinism. I am not aware of a Hebrew word for this concept, but the word comes from to determine in English or determinare in Latin. While the linguistic analysis of the word is not particularly important, the way it is used is. A study of dictionaries and encyclopedias shows that the common denominator in all the definitions of determinism is the contrast between determinism and human free will. Determinism means that human beings' behavior is determined not by our choices, our wills, but by externals factors. From this perspective there is no difference between classical determinism and quantum non-determinism – in both cases everything is determined by material elements in the world, by the materia in the world and the movements of particles from which everything is composed. In a sense, the issue of the existence or non-existence of advance knowledge of the development of matter is secondary. In the classic case, in principle, it is possible to know in advance and to predict the future at every stage of development, while in the quantum scenario, the future cannot be accurately predicted. However, in both cases the movement of materia determines everything in the world and a person's choice plays no part. Hence, the word determinism can be applied to an equal degree to every development that is exclusively determined by the laws of nature.

From a secular perspective that is all that there is: There is materia and there are laws, and everything is determined by the laws of nature and obeys them. There is a tool for investigating, describing and understanding everything that exists in the world, and that tool is science. Science is supposed to explain everything in the world, including man's behavior. Of course science is constantly developing and gradually explaining new phenomena, and if something is not currently explained then it will be at some point in the future. This is the secular belief that is based, as it were, on the outstanding achievements of modern science.

But there are "gaps" in this approach. In particular it is not compatible with the existence of the free will of human beings. But we will put off the discussion of the problem of free will versus the scientific view of the world until the end of the next section, which is dedicated to the concept of free will.

5. Free Will

In the previous section we saw that in a deterministic world, which is governed solely by the laws of nature, the desires of man and his free will are completely foreign. Now let us look in more depth at the concept of free will. It would seem that with the concept of free will there can be no surprises for us – we are used to using both the concept and our free will almost all the time. Our lives are a series of choices and decisions, some of them more important and some of them less so. If my ability to choose is taken away from me then I will cease to be me, I will cease to be a person, and I will cease to be a creative being. I am convinced of this, but philosophers who have dedicated time and effort to the problem of free will have come to the conclusion that there is no logical proof and there can be no experimental proof for the existence of free will, just as there can be no proof of its non-existence. Our knowledge that free will exists is not based on logical inference – it is an immediate human experience.

The concept of free will is a distinctly unscientific one. This means that there is no possibility of defining scientifically what free will is. To define something scientifically is to suggest a way in which one can test it through experiment. Sometimes we make a decision and regret it afterwards, but we do not have the option of going back to the time that we made the decision and deciding differently. We are convinced that we could have made a different decision, a better one, that we had the free will to decide otherwise. However it is impossible to think of an experiment that can either prove or disprove this. In such an experiment we would need to go back to the time that the decision was made and check whether my Self makes the same decision or a different one. We would also need to remove my thoughts about the original, unsuccessful decision, which would unquestionably cause me to change my decision. We do not need to go on with this explanation any further to understand that there is no way of carrying out an experiment which tests the existence of free will.

Furthermore, free will is not compatible with "the scientific picture of the world", and it even contradicts it. According to the scientific picture of the world, the world is governed solely by the laws of nature. This absurd imaginary world has already been described in the previous section. The human body is made up of material components, all of which obey the laws of nature and move in accordance with them. Hence if the laws of nature exclusively determine all the movements of a person's body (like all other things in the world) then there is no room for man's will as an independent being. I should emphasize that we are talking here about a choice between two options which do not contradict the laws of nature – such as to raise my arm or not. Man does not have the choice to fly like a bird or to run like a gazelle – we are talking here about freedom to choose subject to existing constraints. In the next section we will talk in more detail about the relationship between the laws of nature and man's free will.

So how do philosophers who are convinced that there is nothing in the world other than nature and its laws solve this problem? The usual solution is to deny the existence of man's free will, and to say that what I think I have done by choice was actually pre-determined by all sorts of causes that preceded it. My choice is not actually a choice but just an illusion. Einstein, who believed in the determinism of the world, stated his opinion on the subject as follows:

The spatiotemporal laws are complete. This means, there is not a single law of nature that, in principle, could not be reduced to a law within the domain of space-time concepts. This principle implies, for instance, the conviction that psychic entities and relations can be reduced, in the last analysis, to processes of a physical and chemical nature within the nervous system. According to this principle, there are no nonphysical elements in the causal system of the processes of nature. In this sense, there is no room for "free will" in the framework of scientific thought...[17]

However one needs to understand the implications of this radical solution and its price. A person who is convinced that there is no free will is not responsible for his actions. If I am unable to choose according to my own will, if my actions are dictated by the laws of nature, then I am not responsible for them. No court of law can judge a person whose actions are all determined not by him but by the laws of nature – we do not judge a robot. Clearly Einstein himself, in his life, behaved with the responsibility that comes with the free will to choose according to his conscience. So when it became clear that Nazi Germany was likely to be creating a nuclear bomb, Einstein's lack of belief in free will did not prevent him from writing to President Roosevelt in 1939 suggesting that the United States start working on their own nuclear bomb. In a deterministic world, which Einstein believed in, there is no reason for any action, including writing to the president of the United States of America.

From a religious perspective, free will is a matter of faith. Judaism's position is clear: free will is one of the foundations of our faith, and it is firmly rooted in the consciousness of every believing Jew. The principle of free will is a necessary condition for the existence of the Jewish ethical system. As Maimonides writes: "Were a man compelled to act according to the dictates of predestination, then the commands and prohibitions of the Law would become null and void and the Law would be completely false, since man would have no freedom of choice in what he does. Moreover, *it would be useless, in fact absolutely in vain*, for man to study, to instruct, or attempt to learn an art..." (*Eight Chapters*, Chapter Eight). And later, in the same chapter, "In reality, the undoubted truth of the matter is that man has full sway over all his actions. If he wishes to do a thing, he does it; if he does not wish to do it, he need not... God said: See, I have set before

---

17. Physics, Philosophy and Scientific Progress. Journal of the International College of Surgeons, 1950, XIV, 755-758

thee this day life and the good, death and evil...therefore choose life". In the Babylonian Talmud (Brachot 33b) Rabbi Hanina states: "Everything is in the hands of heaven except for the fear of heaven". This means that man is given the freedom to choose to serve God or not to serve God. *Without the infrastructure of free will, Judaism becomes a collection of parables with no normative validity.*

The Midrash relates that the creation of man was a kind of revolution. This man, for whom the entire world was created, at first was not created with a consensus:

At the time that the Holy One, Blessed Be He, came to create Adam, Benevolence said: Create, and Truth said: Don't create. He picked up Truth and cast her to the ground. The ministering angels said: Lord of the World, why do you curse your Truth? While the ministering angels were arguing, God created him. (Bereshit Rabba, 5)

What was the nature of the objection to the creation of man? The entire creation without man functions in complete harmony with the will of the Creator. There is only one corner of creation that is not compelled to act specifically according to the will of the Creator, but is free to act according to its own will. This exceptional case is man, the possessor of choice. Here God is on the brink of bringing into the world a new entity, which is liable to violate the harmony in creation. It is this innovation that arouses the objection to his creation.

The ministering angels saw creation as a perfect composition which could be spoiled by man's involvement. This was not God's intention; He viewed creation as a work that needed completing, as the Torah states: "which God created to make", and the only creature able to complete it is man (not an act of "perfecting" but "completion", according to Rabbi Kook).

Now we return to our discussion of the problem of free will

versus an imaginary world that is governed purely by the laws of nature. One needs to understand that there is a gaping chasm between a "scientific" world that is solely governed by the laws of nature and a world in which alongside the laws of nature, free will is also a factor that can bring about change. To comprehend this we need to put in substantial intellectual efforts and separate ourselves from our routine way of thinking that prevents us from noticing the amazing aspect of reality that is hidden beneath the surface.

We have already mentioned that the concept of free will cannot be explained or described at all using scientific tools. Let us take a look at the following two statements: "Water boils when it is heated to a temperature of one hundred degrees Celsius" and "In August 1986 I was invited to deliver a lecture at the Scientific Institute in Boston. I traveled to Boston and gave the lecture." The first statement is an example of scientific causation: the cause – heating the water to one hundred degrees Celsius (under certain conditions) – brings about the effect – the boiling of the water. This is a general, universal connection – the same cause leads to the same effect – in every place at every time heating water causes it to boil. The generality of this connection enables it to be studied using scientific tools. In contrast, the second statement is about a particular event in my life. Here too there is a cause and effect: the cause – the decision to accept the invitation to give a lecture, the effect – traveling to Boston and giving the lecture. There is nothing scientific in this cause-effect connection, it is a one-off event and cannot be dealt with using scientific tools. But as far as I am concerned, this causal connection is no less real than the scientific connection in the first example. Moreover, I learn about the connection between heating water and it boiling from study and experiments, while I know the causal connection between my decision and its execution in an unmediated way, in my soul. (But it is important to understand that this is not a logical proof for the existence of free will and the causality that is based on it. A determinist could argue that the things that we experience as free will are not actually so, but a result of a chain of causes and effects which began at the creation of the world.)

Hence we have before us two systems of causation that differ in purpose, nature and source. According to the secular view there is only one system of causation, it is the laws of nature, and hence the basic fact of free will seems mysterious. But we are witnesses in our lives to free will both in large and small matters. It is expressed in the important life decisions that we make, such as whether to move to Israel or to become more observant – decisions that we only make very rarely, and in the decisions that we make all the time – whether to read this book or another one, to listen to the news, to go out for a walk and generally to perform any kind of action – standing up, walking, sitting, turning to the left or the right and the like.

I should point out that free will is a prerequisite for creativity, a trait which distinguishes human beings from other creatures on Earth. It is clear that without the ability to choose between different options one cannot produce creative works. Without free will there is no creativity. It must be that free will lies at the very core of human existence.

The existence of the causal system that is connected to free will is expressed in the fact that it is completely impossible to scientifically predict the behavior of human beings. Scientific tools can be used for systems that do not have a connection with the spirit – such as the heavenly bodies, and machines and devices that are based on the use of the laws of physics – such as lasers, radios and televisions. An ordinary sane person who is not involved in philosophical ruminations has absolutely no doubt about the existence of his own free will. But despite this, it is impossible to logically or scientifically prove the existence, or the non-existence, of the phenomenon of free will.

One can look at the relationship between the system of scientific causation and the system of causation of free will from another perspective. In the process of the development of the world (see below in Chapters Four and Five) new entities were created, each one at a higher level than the one before it. So, immediately after the creation of the world there was only raw matter – the inanimate world, and thereafter entities were created that were on higher levels – plant, animal and then man. They do not appear as part of the developmental continuum, but as a jump from one level to the next.[18] The inanimate world is governed by the laws of physics (as a part of the divine governance that exists at all the levels), and at the higher levels the laws of physics act together with other properties that distinguish the new entity. With animals it is their system of instincts that determines their behavior, but their bodies are made from matter – and hence the laws of physics are also acting upon them.

Now let us take a look at man. We presented him in Chapter One as the most complex and sophisticated creature on Earth, in whom many levels of being exist side by side. His body is a material system and the laws of physics control it;

---

18. This is what Daniel Shalit explains in his book *Heaven and Earth*. He points out the lack of continuity, the jumps between the inanimate and plants, animals and humans: from a physical-chemical mechanism to a living organism, and from there to consciousness and the free human Self.

at a higher level his instincts can affect his behavior – he too is an animal. But he also has a soul, with self-awareness and free will. This is his highest level, which brings him close to God. The difficulty in explaining and defining free will using scientific-physical concepts and terminology that belong to the low, basic level is clear. Above, we cited Einstein's opinion, that there is no room for free will in the framework of scientific thought, but there is also no room in that framework for the instincts that exist in the animal kingdom. If animals were able to think and to perform logical analysis, they would claim that as far as they were concerned, in their framework of thinking there is no room for free will. Only man is capable of grasping the concept of free will, but he cannot define it in terms of the lower levels within him. Therefore we can understand the difficulty in understanding free will from a secular perspective which insists on a scientific description of all of reality.

6. Free Will and the Openness of the World to the Will of Man and Divine Providence

In the previous section we came to the understanding that as well as scientific causality there is also a system of causality that is connected to free will. But it is important to understand that the physical world is not closed, it is open to man's will – as only then can free will be realized. Also, recognizing the lofty, transcendental nature of God should not cause us to ignore the issue of providence, of the involvement of God in the affairs of the world, both the physical world and the spiritual world. Our focus in this section will be understanding the openness of the physical world to the will of man. Man was created in God's image and likeness: "Let us make mankind in our image, after our likeness..." (Genesis 1:26). Clearly it is important to understand the openness of the world to God. But we, human beings, do not have the tools to study providence. Nevertheless we can hope that understanding the openness of nature to the will of man will help us to comprehend, even if only in a limited and partial way, the issue of providence.

We have seen that when the laws of nature exclusively govern everything in the world, there is no room for man's will and for God's involvement. Therefore, the question for which we need to find an answer is under which conditions can the laws of nature and the wills of human beings act together? A car travels on a road, acts and moves in accordance with the laws of physics, but ultimately its path is determined by the person at the wheel. Similarly, a person's movements are determined by the laws of nature, but not solely by them – man's will also governs his actions.

We saw in Chapter One that the interaction between matter and spirit, the reciprocal relationship between the body and the soul, is one of the great wonders of the world. We are incapable of understanding how man's will and the laws of nature work alongside each other. Nevertheless, *we can examine whether the laws of physics are compatible with the existence of free will*. We saw in Chapter Two, section 1 that the laws of physics are a reflection of the laws of nature – part of the order of the world, and we believe that God created them as one of the tools of His providence. It is clear, therefore, that the laws of nature must be compatible with man's free will and with divine intervention.

We, human beings, do not have direct access to the divine laws of nature, but physics provides us with these laws at varying approximations. In this section we will examine whether the laws of physics are compatible with man's will. In physics we have two types of laws – the deterministic laws of classical physics which determine all development in advance, and the non-deterministic laws of quantum physics. Let us ask ourselves the following question: What distinguishes the movement of the human body from the movement of inanimate objects, such as the planets? The movements of the human body are determined not only by the laws of physics but also by man's will. I should stress that man's decisions are not the derivatives of any laws of nature but are an independent cause over and above the laws of nature. This gives rise to the next condition of the compatibility between the laws of physics and free will: *A physical system can move in a way that is not in accordance with particular laws, without violating the laws of physics.* The first part of the condition states that a physical object can move in a way that is "not according to the law" without obeying any law, like movements that are determined by man's choices, and the second part states that in these movements there are no violations of the laws of physics. Sounds odd? Soon we will see that this is, in fact, possible. All of man's limbs and organs are made of matter, and hence the human body is a physical system. We have seen that this physical system is capable of moving not only according to certain laws, such as the laws of nature – man's will also affects its movements. On the other hand, it is not possible that every time we carry out our will there are violations of the laws of nature. From our perspective, the laws of nature are a divine command, and, with all the developments of man and the world, they do not change.

Now we can go back to the two types of laws that we defined earlier, and check which of them fulfills the condition stated above. It is clear that classical physics with its deterministic laws does not fulfill the condition for compatibility with free will. Let us look at the human body – if the deterministic laws of classical physics control a person's body, and his position at a particular time is known, and all the physical forces acting upon him are also known, then his movements will be determined from now onwards, and free will has no place.[19] So we have come to the conclusion that the laws of classical physics, including the theory of relativity, do not allow for free will. In a system of completely deterministic laws, when all the movements of a physical body are pre-determined, no spiritual entity is able to affect them.

---

19. It is clear that our knowledge of the position of the body and the forces acting on it are not important at all; what is important is that they exist.

Conversely, modern physics, which also includes quantum theory, is compatible with the existence of free will. The movements of single quantum particles are not determined by any law. Quantum theory does not provide predictions for the movements of a single particle; it only gives likelihoods, possibilities, chances that can only be tested in an experiment involving large groups of particles, but not in any experiment with just a lone particle. Hence we can say that the quantum particle *can move in a way that is not in accordance with certain laws without violating the laws of physics.* The laws of physics relate not to a single particle, but to groups of many particles. In other words, the movements of the quantum particle fulfill the condition that we set out above. However, this claim is not an answer to the question of whether free will is compatible with the laws of physics. The human body is not a quantum particle, but a macroscopic system that contains many particles. Hence, we need to bring an example of a macroscopic system that is affected by non-deterministic quantum laws. If a macroscopic object such as a human body can carry out arbitrary movements without contravening the laws of physics, only then can we say that free will is compatible with physical lawfulness.

Let us take a look at the movement of a spaceship in outer space. We shall assume that we know the spaceship's speed at a particular time and place, as well as the gravitational field at every point along its path. Then, according to the laws of mechanics we can predict the spaceship's path with great accuracy. If we input all the data, including the laws of mechanics, into a computer, we can obtain the data of the spaceship's path and the observation of the spaceship's movement will confirm our prediction. Suddenly, something happens and the spaceship starts to move in an unexpected way without any coordination and bearing no relation to the predictions. How can this be? Are the laws of mechanics wrong? This is impossible – innumerable experiments have been performed that confirm the laws of mechanics! The laws of mechanics are correct. The spaceship's deviation from its path is due to the fact that the person inside it has started to steer it.

Now we will bring an example of how a spaceship can deviate from its path not because of a human cause but also because of quantum processes that influence its movement. Let us imagine that on top of the spaceship is a Geiger counter – a device that reacts to lone (cosmic) particles that attack any object in outer space in a completely random way. Let us assume that every time a cosmic particle hits the Geiger counter, the spaceship changes its direction by a particular angle. Let us also assume that the direction of the deviation and the increase in the speed of the spaceship are determined by the energy and speed (or momentum) of the particle that hits the Geiger counter (from a physical perspective this is absolutely possible). As a result, it would seem to an external observer that the spaceship is behaving like a drunk, randomly changing direction. In this example, the path of the spaceship cannot be scientifically predicted even though the spaceship is moving in accordance with the laws of physics. How is this possible? Surely macroscopic objects have to comply with the deterministic laws of classical physics. The difference is that in this example quantum processes affect the movements of the object. If there were quantum processes in our brains affecting our behavior, we would all behave like drunks. In this model the spaceship is not a closed system but is affected by cosmic particles external to it. However, it would not be difficult to come up with a model of a closed spaceship that can be affected by random quantum processes. To do this one would need to place the source of the particles inside the spaceship. Then the spaceship would make the same movements but it would be a completely closed physical system.

We have brought here an example of a macroscopic system which fulfills the condition of compatibility of the laws of physics with free will: The physical system can move in a way that is not in accordance with certain laws without violating the laws of physics. We have shown that the laws of modern physics are compatible with the principle of free will. The physical world, the world of matter, is not closed but is open to the involvement of God and man. There is interaction between matter and spirit. The spirit can affect the movements of matter not only through the established spiritual system, that is the laws of nature, but also by the constant providence over the movements and by the will of man. It became clear to us that not every system of physical laws meets the condition of openness to the intervention of the spirit. The classic deterministic laws do not fulfill this condition, whereas the laws of modern physics are compatible with it. However, we do not have to rely on the nature of the physical laws that are known to us at this time. The famous philosopher Immanuel Kant was unable to solve the problem of free will because of his belief in the deterministic nature of the laws of classical mechanics. *But our belief does not have to be subject to the state of our knowledge at any given time.*

The openness of the material world to the intervention of God and man is a metaphysical, religious principle which derives from the Torah. It is a wonderful thing that science has reached the stage where it is compatible with this principle, but this is not a "scientific" proof of the metaphysical principle that lies at the foundation of Judaism. I would say that the principle of the openness of the material world is a metaphysical principle of all the sciences, and if classical physics does not comply with this principle then this points to a flaw in classical physics (in its description of the laws, not in the laws themselves), but it does not prevent us from using classical physics at a certain approximation and within certain limits.

Thus we have come to an astonishing conclusion, that the laws of nature are compatible with God's involvement and with man's will in the world. To put it another way, the existence of the laws of nature does not contradict the involvement of God and man in matters of the world, but is compatible with them. *Nature, the physical world, is open to the supernatural influence of God and man.*

Let us now return to the argument. We have mentioned that according to the secular view man is part of nature, and his behavior and thoughts must all obey the laws of nature only, and the existence of any supernatural entity is denied. According to this view, man's free will and creativity are a mystery and a miracle that cannot have a rational explanation. On the other hand, according to the more extreme (and more consistent) secular view there is no mystery. There is simply no such thing as free will, and the feeling of freedom that we have is simply an illusion that comes from our lack of knowledge of all the causes that brought us to our decisions, whatever they may be. Either way, human behavior is a gap or deficiency in the fabric of secular thought. The denial of the existence of free will leads us to a serious contradiction: How is it possible to talk about basic human freedoms and rights when man's most fundamental freedom – free will – is denied? We have seen in this chapter that the non-deterministic structure of modern physics is compatible with the involvement of the spirit in the movement of matter.

CHAPTER THREE: KNOWLEDGE OF THE WORLD

1. Scientific Knowledge

Now we shall focus on a very important subject – scientific knowledge. In this chapter we shall address the following questions: What is the source of scientific theories? Can the truth of a scientific theory and its conclusions be proved? What are the limitations of science in describing our world? This subject is of supreme importance. One of the goals of our discussion is to pull the rug out from under the feet of the notion, popular amongst laymen, scientists and philosophers, that the world can be explained scientifically, without God.

What is science? What is the structure of science? And how is it different from philosophy, the purpose of which is also to describe and explain the world? The structure of science is very similar to that of mathematics – at its basis lie premises, and the laws of science are intended to reflect, embody and symbolize the laws of nature to a certain approximation. In contrast with philosophy which claims to describe everything, the goal of science is to describe only matter. Another issue is that there are philosophers who claim that nature is the source of everything, including man and his soul, but this is not a scientific claim, it is an arbitrary philosophical assumption. In contrast with the philosophical premises that cannot be confirmed or refuted either by logic or experience, the scientific laws of nature can be tested through experiments.

We have said that the structure of scientific theory is very similar to the structure of mathematics. At the basis of the theory lie its premises, which are the laws of science, themselves reflections of the true laws of nature. The laws of science are mathematical equations (like axioms) from which conclusions can be drawn (like theorems) which can be tested by experiment. So, using the fundamental equations of Newton's law of gravity it is possible to calculate the paths of the Earth and other heavenly bodies around the sun, and using astronomic observations it is possible to test whether these calculations are correct. A contradiction between the observational data and the predicted data indicates a flaw in the theory, while if the two sets of data are the same, the theory is supported and corroborated but not proven to be true. It could still happen that observations of other bodies will contradict the theory.

We have therefore come to an interesting conclusion: An experiment can corroborate a scientific theory, but it cannot prove it absolutely, since it is not inconceivable that there may be experiments that contradict it or that there will be such experiments in the future, and it is fundamentally impossible to carry out all the possible experiments, including the future ones, to be convinced of the truth of the theory. It is impossible to verify the premises of the laws of science through experience, and therefore it is impossible to prove the truth of a scientific theory through experience. There is a significant difference between the status of philosophical premises and that of the premises of a scientific theory: One can prove the incorrectness of a scientific theory, or *refute* it, by experiment, while philosophical premises can neither be proven nor refuted. Soon we shall see that this difference between philosophy and science is crucial.

Now we shall turn to the central question of the theory of scientific knowledge: From where can human beings infer the laws of nature, or their reflections – the laws of science – which are the premises of science? Many people, including scientists, do not see the question of scientific knowledge as an especially difficult one. They believe that the scientific theories and the laws of nature can be derived and inferred from the findings of experiments and observations; that is to say, we know the world through our five senses. Experimental data, together with logical inference are sufficient for us to arrive at the laws of nature and to formulate them. This approach, *from the particular to the general*, from experiment to theory, is called *induction*. One should not be alarmed by this word – it is simply a short way of saying: *the drawing of conclusions from the particular to the general*. The opposite process, the *drawing of conclusions from the general to the particular*, is called *logical inference* or *deduction*. The basis of *induction* is the principle that it is possible to infer the general – a scientific theory or a law of nature – from the particular, from experimental results and observations. Scientists are not necessarily experts in the theory of cognition, and in general they believe in induction. Moreover, Bertrand Russell, one of the great philosophers of the twentieth century, claimed that science could not discover the laws of nature without the principle of induction, since if knowledge does not come from experiments then where does it come from? On the other hand, it is clear that from a limited collection of data it is impossible to infer a theory that includes an infinite amount of information.

In fact, in the eighteenth century, the Scottish philosopher David Hume proved that the principle of induction has no validity and is, in fact, erroneous. In his book *Treatise of Human Nature*, he proves that it is impossible to infer laws of nature from experiments. In his opinion, induction has no substance, and no logical argument can prove that "the incidents about which we have no experience are similar to those for which we have experience." This means that "even observation of a regular or fixed combination of objects cannot infer anything about any object beyond our experience." *In other words, we cannot infer any theory from experience.* Of course, when we say that we cannot infer theories from experience, we mean that we cannot construct theories in a rational way, using logical processes, based on observable data alone.

But this is not all that convincing. In general, people, including scientists, rely on simple examples of recurring events, such as the movement of the hands of a clock. One only has to take a look at an ordinary clock to come to the unequivocal conclusion that the second hand will change its position on the clock face every second, and to predict the positions of all the hands on the clock for a long period of time. So, on the basis of a short experiment – a quick look at a clock – we come to a theoretical conclusion, to a theory that enables us to predict the positions of the hands for an apparently unlimited period of time. Let us look at another example: the transitions between night and day that we witness on a daily basis. From our observations, we very easily come to the conclusion that this cycle will continue in the future.

These examples, and we could come up with countless similar examples, do not contradict Hume's conclusion that it is impossible to derive, logically, by a formal proof, from a particular observation, a theory that describes the behavior of an object over an unlimited period of time. In simple cases it is relatively easy to assume and guess that the future will not be different from the past. The claim that the cycle of day and night will continue for an unlimited amount of time is not a conclusion that results logically from observational data – it is a guess, an assumption, a hypothesis, that we posit regarding the future behavior of the object. This hypothesis can be corroborated or refuted by further observations, but we will never be able to verify it absolutely. To do this we would need to carry out an infinite number of experiments, and even these would not entirely verify the hypothesis; they would simply reinforce it. Incidentally, in the examples that we have brought, the assumption that the repetitive behavior will continue for an unlimited period of time is actually not correct. The clock will stop when the battery runs out. And the cycle of day and night will stop when the sun's thermonuclear reactor is extinguished.

In contrast to these simple examples, the scientist aims to discover the fundamental laws of nature. Here we realize that Hume's discovery is not simply an abstract philosophical claim that has no connection to reality, but actually has practical implications. In the cases above we tried to predict whether a particular behavior would continue – the repetitive movement of the hands of a clock or the cycle of day and night, but we did not even try to discover the laws that determine these movements. A look at a clock says nothing about the mechanism that is responsible for the movement of its hands. Similarly, by observing the cycle of day and night it is impossible to say anything about the law of gravity and Newtonian mechanics.

Generally speaking, there is no similarity between the data from a particular experiment or from a series of experiments, and the fundamental law that the experiment is intended to comply with. When, in 1915, Albert Einstein completed his formulation of the general theory of relativity, he defined three phenomena that arose from his theory. One of these phenomena was a prediction of the deflection of a ray of light that "grazes" the sun. In 1919 an experiment was performed during a solar eclipse which supported this prediction – the deflection of a ray of light by 1.75 arc-seconds. This was the result of the experiment, but there is not even a hint of similarity between this result and Einstein's equations that describe a change in the curvature of space-time over time.

Einstein writes about the general theory of relativity in his autobiography: "I have learned something else from the theory of gravitation: No ever so inclusive collection of empirical facts can ever lead to the setting up of such complicated equations. A theory can be tested by experience, *but there is no way from experience to the setting up of a theory.*"[1]

---

1. Autobiographical Notes in *Albert Einstein: Philosopher-Scientist*, Paul Arthur Schilpp, p. 89

The denial of the theory of induction is a serious problem for the theory of scientific cognition. How is it possible to arrive at the laws of nature if not by inferring from the results of our observations? Bertrand Russell expresses his opinion on this in a colorful way:

[Hume] arrives at the disastrous conclusion that from experience and observation nothing is to be learnt. There is no such thing as a rational belief... The lunatic who believes that he is a poached egg is to be condemned solely on the ground that he is in a minority... This is a desperate point of view, and it must be hoped that there is some way of escaping from it.[2]

The laws of science that reflect the laws of nature are mathematical equations. Earlier (Chapter Two, section 2) I brought some examples of these equations – Maxwell's equations that describe the electromagnetic field and Einstein's equations that describe the gravitational field. As we have seen, no experiment produces these texts, and these equations are not written anywhere in nature. We have shown that it is impossible to infer these equations from any observation or experiment, or from pure logic or intellectual contemplation. However, great scientists such as Isaac Newton, James Clerk Maxwell and Albert Einstein have discovered these equations. The question that we need to address is how it is possible for science to exist at all, if it is impossible to infer its premises either from experience or from logic. How have the world's great scientists managed to come up with the fundamental equations of science? These are questions that belong to the theory of scientific cognition, and we shall address them in the following sections.

In the next section we shall see how secular thought deals with the problem of scientific cognition.

---

2. Bertrand Russell, A History of Western Philosophy, pp. 672-3

2. Secular Solutions to the Problem of Scientific Cognition

On March 14, 1879, in the city of Ulm in Germany, a baby was born into a fairly assimilated Jewish family, and he was given a German name, Albert. When a baby boy is born, the parents often think about their hopes and visions for their son's future. But even in their wildest dreams, young Albert's parents could not have imagined that their son would be one of the most famous people in the world, that he would change the face of modern physics and that he would start a veritable scientific revolution – in short, that he would be Albert Einstein. He discovered *new* scientific theories that did not follow from the scientific theories that previous scientists had already discovered. This was something completely new, which was not latent in any object of human culture that had accumulated over the thousands of years before Einstein's revolutionary discoveries.

Where can new human knowledge come from, when all the sources of knowledge are either in man's soul or in his cultural environment? The new theories that Einstein discovered did not previously exist in human culture, and we cannot assume that baby Albert was born with these theories already in his soul (if this was the case, then it would be a supernatural phenomenon that would be impossible to explain without the involvement of some kind of supernatural force). It would seem that there is a simple solution to the problem of new knowledge, and that is the principle of induction: The scientist discovers the laws of nature by observation and experiment; the data from these observations and experiments and the logical analysis of these data lead the scientist to a formulation of the laws of nature. In fact, as we mentioned, many scientists and some philosophers believe that this is the only way to discover the laws of nature, and we cited earlier the philosopher Bertrand Russell who was convinced that without the principle of induction science could not exist.

However, in the previous section we saw that this principle is invalid and David Hume proved this back in the eighteenth century. In the next section we shall see that new knowledge comes to the world by divine revelation. But how do secular philosophers, who do not rely on divine revelation, explain the creation of new knowledge in the world? It would seem that a coherent secular approach is not capable of providing a solution to this problem and comes to an unequivocal conclusion: the appearance of new knowledge is a miracle, and the intelligibility of the world is a mystery.

So let us focus on an analysis of the secular solutions to the problem of the principle of induction: If it is impossible to infer the laws of nature from nature, how can we explain the existence of science and all of its discoveries? This question occupied Immanuel Kant (1724-1804), the eminent German philosopher. For twelve years Kant tried to solve Hume's problem. If it is impossible to logically derive a scientific theory from experience, as Hume showed, how is it possible to determine it at all? How do the laws of science exist when they cannot be derived from experience? And furthermore, Kant was certain that the laws of science, namely Newtonian mechanics, are proven, that they are the absolute truth, and all that needs to be done is to find a way to discover them. After twelve years it took Kant only a few months to formulate a solution to the problem.

Kant's solution was somewhat odd, and difficult to understand. In my book, *Law and Providence*, I devoted a fair amount of time to a critique of Kant's theory of cognition. I shall lay out the main conclusions here without going into the reasoning behind them. Kant actually cultivated a worldview that espouses a man-centered universe. It is not God but man who determines ethics, what is right and wrong, and Kant even came to the paradoxical conclusion that man also determines the laws of nature. Hume showed that it is impossible to derive the laws of nature from an observation of it. But the fact is that science exists. Where does it come from? The only option, when we ignore the existence of God, is to say that man determines the laws of nature.

Kant's general idea is that it is the human intellect that invents its laws and imposes them on the raw material in the experiment. Mankind grasps these laws a priori, prior to the experiment and without any connection to it. "The understanding does not derive its laws (a priori) from, but prescribes them, to nature."[3] These laws, which are not the outcomes of experiment, organize the raw data of the experiment. These laws are claims – general, universal statements – that we assume about the world of the experiment. As I have already said, I do not intend to reproduce here Kant's complex and convoluted argument that seemingly supports his conclusions. In Law and Providence I showed the flaws in Kant's reasoning, with the help of the arguments of other philosophers. Here I shall mention only Einstein's attitude towards Kant's theory of cognition, and I shall bring two quotations from Einstein. In one, Einstein explains why the comprehensibility of the world is a mystery and he criticizes Kant's "solution" to this mystery. This is what he wrote in his Letter to Solovine:

You find it remarkable that the comprehensibility of the world...seems to me a wonder or eternal secret. Now, a priori, one should, after all, expect a chaotic world that is in no way graspable through thinking. One could (even should) expect that the world turns out to be lawful only insofar as we make an ordering intervention. It would be a kind of ordering like putting into alphabetic order the words of a language [as Kant presents his theory of knowledge]. On the other hand, the kind of order which, for example, was created through [the discovery] of Newton's theory of gravitation is of quite a different character. Even if the axioms of the theory are put forward by human agents, *the success of such an enterprise*

---

3.   Kant, Prolegomena, p. 67

does suppose a high degree of order in the objective world, which one had no justification whatever to expect a priori. Here lies the sense of "wonder" which increases even more with the development of our knowledge.[4]

Elsewhere Einstein emphasizes that there is no basis to Kant's claim that man produces certain knowledge about the laws of nature from his intellect:

If, therefore, we have definitely assured knowledge, it must be grounded in reason itself. This is held to be the case, for example, in the propositions of geometry and in the principle of causality. These and certain other types of knowledge are, so to speak, a part of the implements of thinking and therefore do not previously have to be gained from sense data (i.e., they are a priori knowledge). *Today everyone knows, of course, that these concepts do not have the certainty or internal necessity that Kant attributed to them.*[5]

Kant's philosophy in general, and his theory of cognition in particular, have influenced many philosophers and continue to do so today. As we have said, he established his worldview of a man-centered universe without any reference to God (despite the fact that he himself believed in God). While his theory of cognition is still fairly popular, many philosophers realize that it is incorrect. To understand this one just needs to see that Kant claimed that Newton's mechanics and his law of gravity are the absolute, proven truth and he "proved" that that they are the necessary result of human reason, and the final word in their field. But then along came Einstein with a more precise theory, which predicts new phenomena and presents a new scientific worldview, a real revolution. Today it is fair to assume that Einstein's theory is also simply a better approximation to reality, and that in the future a new theory might appear that will be even closer to the truth. Essentially, Einstein is saying this: Today everyone knows, of course, that these concepts do not have the certainty or internal necessity that Kant attributed to them.

---

4. Letters to Solovine 30.III.52

5. Ideas and Opinions, p. 22

The scientific revolution brought with it a new understanding of the status of a scientific theory – it is not absolute knowledge, as Kant thought, but an estimate, a guess, a hypothesis that describes reality to a particular approximation. It is important to note that even in Kant's time there was a philosopher who understood this. Solomon Maimon (1754-1800) wrote in a private letter to Kant that both Newton's mechanics and Kant's theory are simply hypotheses. In reply, Kant wrote that Maimon was a "parasite, like all Jews"[6].

Thus, scientific theory does not have the status of absolute truth, it has the status of a hypothesis that describes reality to a certain approximation. This insight led Karl Popper in the twentieth century to formulate his theory of cognition as follows:

a. As David Hume proved, it is impossible to infer scientific laws from observations, *from the particular to the general*; namely, the principle of induction does not exist.

b. At the foundation of a scientific theory are the laws of science, which are the premises, the axioms of the theory. From these we infer the results of the theory that can be tested by experiments. The scientific theory has a deductive structure, of inferring conclusions *from the general to the particular*.

c. How do we come up with the premises of the theory, the scientific laws? How do we come up with the scientific theories? Popper's answer to this question is fairly straightforward. *We have to see all theories as hypotheses, as estimates (that is, as guesses).* These theories are man-made. They are nothing but premises that cannot be inferred from experience. *The structure of science is deductive – from the general to the particular.*

How does science develop? The new theories refute the previous theo-

---

6. Joseph Agassi, The History of Modern Philosophy, 278

ries and leave them with a limited scope of application. But the new physical theories, such as the special and general theory of relativity and quantum theory, are only hypotheses, estimates, guesses. This therefore raises the question: Are there rational arguments or experiments that can give preference to one hypothesis over the other? Karl Popper's answer is as follows: No scientific theory can be *verified* by experiment. In order to prove a theory an infinite number of experiments has to be conducted, including future experiments, which is clearly impossible. An increased number of experiments can only *strengthen* the scientific theory, but they cannot *prove that it is true.*

There were many experiments whose results were compatible with Newton's mechanics and his law of gravity, and which did not contradict them, but in the twentieth century Albert Einstein discovered new theories and predicted new phenomena which contradicted the conclusions of Newtonian mechanics and the law of gravity. It is impossible to prove a theory, which is simply a hypothesis, an estimate, a guess, since it does not matter how many experiments corroborate it, there is no guarantee that tomorrow a new experiment will not appear that contradicts it. The only way, according to Popper, to choose one hypothesis over another is by refuting one of them. The refutation of any theory is possible by the contradiction, either theoretical or experimental, of the deductive implications of the theory (the implications that are arrived at by logical inference). This can be done with only a few experiments or even just one. A scientific theory, until it is refuted, remains a hypothesis, an estimate, but it is still superior to a theory that has already been refuted.

Popper's solution to the problem of scientific cognition is based on guesses that are discovered by geniuses. These hypotheses (theories) are not necessarily correct; they could be, and it is even very reasonable to assume that they will be, replaced by new theory-hypotheses which will themselves be just guesses.

However, Popper's view, just like Kant's, does not touch on the essence of the problem of scientific cognition and does not provide an answer to it. For us, the problem is about man's ability to discover the laws of nature. Karl Popper does not even profess to deal with this problem. In fact, an analysis of the essence of scientific cognition brings him to the paradoxical conclusion that it (cognition) is impossible: "...[E]ven on the assumption (which I share) that our quest for knowledge has been successful so far, and that we now know something of our universe, this success becomes miraculously improbable, and therefore inexplicable; for an appeal to an endless series of improbable accidents is not an explanation."[7] There is no theory that is capable of explaining why our search for the laws of nature is successful: "Successful explanation must retain...the probability zero, assuming that we measure this probability, approximately, by the ratio of the 'successful' explanatory hypotheses to all hypotheses which might be designed by man."[8]

In this section we have summarized the secular approach to knowledge of the world. From a secular perspective, the fact that we know the world is a mystery. As far as the secular thinker is concerned, knowledge of the world in general and of the laws of nature in particular is a wonder and a mystery. Karl Popper, who was a staunch supporter of the secular view – the study of the world ignoring the existence of God – wrote: "The phenomenon of human knowledge is no doubt the greatest miracle in our universe."[9] Albert Einstein expressed a similar contention: "The eternal mystery of the world is its comprehensibility... The fact that it is comprehensible is a miracle."[10]

---

7. K. R. Popper, Objective Knowledge, p. 28

8. K. R. Popper, Conjectures and Refutations, p. 96

9. Objective Knowledge, VII

10. Ideas and Opinions, p. 292

It is interesting that science and its accomplishments are viewed by the followers of secularism as the stronghold of the secular approach. It is quite ironic that a consistent philosophical examination leads to the conclusion that in the framework of secular thought science cannot exist, and that the phenomenon of science is a miracle for which there is no rational explanation. This is a further gap in the fabric of secular thought.

3. The Nature of Scientific Discovery

We opened the previous section with a story about a baby that was born, just like any other baby, except that when he grew up he brought new knowledge to humankind, knowledge which did not stem from anything that existed prior to that time. Albert studied at school and university and during that time he accumulated a large amount of knowledge in the fields of mathematics and physics. Over a period of eleven years, from 1905 to 1916, Albert Einstein published articles that changed the face of modern physics. These articles brought to the world new concepts and ideas – new knowledge that was not included in the books from which Einstein had studied mathematics and physics, and that was not mentioned in the lectures that he had attended at university. It was completely new knowledge which was not included in any human store of knowledge and which did not follow logically from anything that was known previously.

From the point of view of the secular approach which believes that nature – and man within it, together with the world of the animal, vegetable and the inanimate – is all that there is in the world, there is a problem understanding where new knowledge comes from. If all that exists is man and nature, then it would be reasonable to think that man acquires the new knowledge about nature and its laws from nature, through observations and experiments. But in the previous sections we saw that in the eighteenth century David Hume proved that it is impossible to infer a scientific theory from experiments and observations. Therefore, a consistent secular approach leads us to the conclusion that a new scientific theory can only be reached by way of a miracle! Both Einstein and Popper point this out (see the excerpts at the end of the previous section). This was also a problem for Immanuel Kant, but when a secular philosopher uses the concept of a miracle in reference to something, this is most likely an admission of his inability to understand or explain it.

From a secular perspective, knowing and understanding the world is a mystery that is impossible to explain rationally. We saw above that this is not the only mystery in the secular worldview, and we shall see later that this view of the world contains countless mysteries, which can be solved if we take into account the existence of God. The problem of new knowledge is solved if we assume that both man and nature are open to God. When man's soul is open to God, the mystery of the comprehensibility of the world is solved: there is a source of the new knowledge – it comes from God, the source of all knowledge.

Now we shall turn to the problem of the discovery of the laws of nature. As we explained in Chapter Two, section 2, the laws of nature are part of the divine spiritual world which operates the material world, and without which matter could not exist. The laws of nature are part of the spiritual world and they are one of the tools through which divine providence governs the world. It is important to stress that the laws of nature are only one of the tools of providence. In Chapter Two, section 4, we saw where the arbitrary assumption that it is solely the laws of nature that govern the world leads us. It leads us to a physical world without spirit, populated by robots. Through the divine spiritual world God governs the world and humankind within it.

Let us summarize: Human beings are not able to arrive at scientific theories from the material world; the laws of nature are not written there, but rather the source of the laws of nature is in the spiritual world. Here the following question arises: How is man able to reveal the laws of nature (to a certain approximation) in the spiritual world? Man grasps the material world through his senses, but they only sense material things – they do not sense any spiritual entity. But nevertheless man has the amazing ability to connect to the spiritual world of human culture, and is thereby able to introduce into his own personal memory a part of the collective memory of humankind.

In Chapter Two, section 2, we defined the concept of the accessible spiritual world, which is part of the spiritual world as a whole. The spiritual world includes within it the laws of nature that have not yet been discovered, while the accessible spiritual world contains only things that are known at a given time. From the moment of its publication a new creation starts to be accessible to all of humankind. We have become accustomed to this accessibility and do not regard it as the slightest bit strange, even though it is in fact an extremely remarkable thing. A long time ago, maybe hundreds of years ago, a certain composer wrote a piece of music and it became part of human culture, and today every person has access to it. Anyone who listens to this musical piece has a unique experience. He is able to feel and experience the musical piece just like the composer himself, and sometimes in an even deeper way. This is a spiritual experience which has no physical sensation. A person can hear a piece of music or read the musical notes, but his experience is not sensory. The connection to the accessible spiritual world which was created by different people at different times is a unique human attribute which distinguishes man from all other creatures.

It is difficult to comprehend the connection to the accessible spiritual world which contains all the knowledge amassed for the benefit of humanity by masterminds in their chosen fields, such as art and science. However, it is considerably harder to comprehend the pioneering act of discovering the secrets hidden in the divine spiritual world. We are talking here about the discovery of new laws, about the formation of science. The spiritual world is not fully open to us, but from time to time new parts of it are revealed to a select few. Maimonides wrote that the processes of knowledge are similar in the divine sciences and the natural sciences. "You should not think that these great *secrets* are fully and completely known to anyone among us. They are not. But sometimes truth flashes out to us so that we think that it is day, and then matter and habit in their various forms conceal it so that we find ourselves again in an obscure night, almost as we were at first. We are like someone in a very dark night over whom lightning flashes time and time again."[11] The spiritual world is not open to us in its entirety, but from time to time new parts of it are revealed to humanity by great prophets, scholars, philosophers, artists and scientists.

Let us continue with Maimonides' metaphor. The parts of the spiritual world that are still not open to human beings are steeped in darkness. On very rare occasions, to select individuals, great scientists and geniuses, a flash of brilliance comes, just like lightning in the dead of night that illuminates the entire sky. But it is important to understand that man has to be ready to receive the flash of light. An ordinary person who is exposed to the revelations of the theory of relativity probably would not understand a thing. Only a person equipped with a great deal of knowledge can grasp it. But as we have already noted, while it is necessary to have a great deal of knowledge, this is not sufficient. It is not man who determines how and when areas of the spiritual world that have remained in darkness will be revealed to him. This is a matter of divine providence.

A consequence of all this is that there are two ways to connect to the spiritual world – a direct, primary connection and an indirect, secondary connection. The divine spiritual world includes, amongst other things, the

---

11. *Guide of the Perplexed*, Introduction, p. 7

laws of nature which constitute part of the divine operating system. God reveals the laws of nature to human beings in a gradual way, and with a particular degree of accuracy, in accordance with the level of knowledge and the intellectual level at the time of the revelation. This revelation occurs not to humanity as a whole, but to a particular individual, to a particular scientist. Many scientists are qualified, in terms of their level of knowledge, to receive the revelation but only a few chosen geniuses actually receive the flash of revelation. It is thus that the laws of nature were revealed to Isaac Newton, to James Clerk Maxwell and to Albert Einstein. Their scientific discoveries are examples of a direct and primary connection to the divine spiritual world; it is not a voluntary action on the part of the scientist but rather an example of divine providence.

One may get the impression from this description that only the scientist-geniuses who discover the new laws of nature receive the flashes of revelation that reveal new areas in the accessible spiritual world. If that is the case, what about the great innovators who have brought to humanity inventions without which we could not imagine our lives, such as the electric light bulb, radio, television, computers, machines, cars, trains and airplanes? Or the mathematicians and scientists who discover new things from the existing theories? The answer is simple: The existing theories contain an infinite amount of information, and, by working systematically, by carrying out a number of logical steps, but without flashes of revelation, it is impossible to arrive at the scrap of information that opens up new, revolutionary opportunities, such as the invention of the wheel.

The problem is that discoveries from the existing theory are contingent not only on the premises of the theory but also on the initial conditions (See Chapter Two, section 1), and there is an infinite number of initial conditions. For example, in the situation described in Figure 1 in Chapter Two, section 1, there is an infinite number of possible speeds and places for the launching of the object. To invent something (in the context of a particular physical theory) means to discover, from the infinite number of possible positions a unique position, a unique configuration of elements of the physical system, that is the invention. It is therefore clear that in order to come up with a great invention from existing theories, divine help is required.

After a new theory, such as the theory of relativity, is published it becomes part of the spiritual world accessible to human beings (Popper's world three). Now, anyone with the requisite level of scientific knowledge can include the theory of relativity in his own spiritual world. This is an example of a secondary connection to the spiritual world. It should be noted that the ability to connect to the spiritual world, whether in a primary or secondary way, is what distinguishes man from all the other creatures on the planet. This quality is linked to man's ability to speak, to his understanding of language and to the documentation of spiritual messages. Every human being has a part in the spiritual world, but people are distinguished from each other in their own spiritual world.

Every human being experiences a secondary connection to the spiritual world; we do this on a regular basis. But the question arises: How does a primary connection to the spiritual world occur for the pioneers of science – the eminent scientists and inventors in the various fields? The famous mathematician Jacques Hadamard conducted a study in which he collected testimonies about innovations in the field of mathematics, a field that is not substantially different from physics. As in the case of physics, in mathematics it is impossible to arrive at laws and innovations via a finite number of logical operations of an existing theory. Thus Gauss, an eminent mathematician, describes how he arrived at a particular arithmetical theorem that he had unsuccessfully tried to prove for years: "Finally, two days ago, I succeeded, not on account of my painful efforts, but by the grace of God. Like a sudden flash of lightning, the riddle happened to be solved. I myself cannot say what was the conducting thread which connected what I previously knew with what made my success possible."[12] The inventor Nicolle writes: "It is like a creation. Contrary to progressive acquirements, such an act owes nothing to logic or to reason. The act of discovery is an accident."[13] The great French mathematician Henri Poincare relates how an important idea came to him as an illumination. Roger Penrose, another great mathematician, relates in his book how a crucial idea in the field of the law of gravity came to him during a short break in a conversation with a friend.[14] The conversation continued and Penrose forgot about the idea, but for the rest of the day he had a feeling of elation and could not understand why, until he recalled the idea that had popped into his head during the earlier conversation.

The common thread in all these testimonies, and others, is that there are two types of processes that lead to a scientific discovery. One is a process of logical operations, of rational thought. One can think about this process as if it is carried out by man's own personal computer – his brain. The second process has absolutely no connection to methodical, logical thought – it is a kind of flash. In contrast to a consistent and logical thought process, the person does not control a process of the second kind. The flash comes to him – it is something that happens to him. It does not happen to everybody, and the person needs to be prepared for it, prepared to be a receptacle. There is a reason why in ancient times there were schools for prophets. A person without scientific training is not capable of making a scientific discovery; the scientific training is only a necessary condition – it is not sufficient. The flash is not dependent on the person, he cannot receive it through a voluntary act.

In this section we discussed the nature of scientific discovery. Neither the phenomenon nor the process of scientific discovery can be understood using the tools of secular

12. J. Hadamard, *The Psychology of Invention in the Mathematical Field*, p. 15

13. Ibid. p. 19

14. R. Penrose, *The Emperor's New Mind*, p. 541

thought. We saw that it is impossible to attain new scientific knowledge from the material world alone, since the laws of nature are part of the spiritual world. But according to secular thought there is no such thing as a spiritual entity that is not dependent on man; the spiritual world is a tool of divine providence which secular thought does not recognize. This is not only true of scientific discovery – any kind of creative work is a foreign concept for the secular approach. Any true creation is unique, and as such it cannot be the subject of scientific study, and the secular approach does not recognize anything that is outside of scientific scrutiny.

In the next section we will look in greater depth at the connection between creativity and divine revelation in Jewish thought.

4. God and Man. Divine Revelation

In Chapter One, we came to the conclusion that it is not possible that a creature as complex and sophisticated as man was formed by itself from the raw matter of the universe. In fact, no object comes into the world without someone creating it; this is all the more true in the case of man. This conclusion fits with our common sense and our accumulated experience. The opposite claim, the secular one, that man was formed spontaneously from nature as it developed has no rational or scientific basis. According to the Jewish-religious worldview, there is a rational source for everything in the world and for the world itself – there is a supreme intellect. In contrast, the atheist view holds that the source of everything is matter that is devoid of both reason and spirituality, and we too are a random result of that same non-rational, material source.

Now let us ask ourselves what we, human beings, know and are capable of knowing, about the creator of the world, other than the fact that He exists. We would expect that the Torah would give us an explicit answer regarding the essence of God, since the Torah is a detailed report of the meeting between man and God. However, contrary to our expectations, the Torah gives us no hint about what God is. The Torah starts with the words "In the beginning God created the heavens and the earth". There is nothing here, and nor is there in the continuation of the story of creation, any explanation of who God is. Furthermore, when Moses asks God his name, and in doing so, his essence, God's response indicates only his existential status, namely his existence in the world: "And God said unto Moses: 'I will be what I will be'; and He said: 'Thus shall you say to the children of Israel: I will be has sent me unto you.'" (Exodus 3:14)

We can understand why the Torah does not tell us about what God is. It is something that human beings are not capable of comprehending – there is a limit to our understanding. It is impossible to grasp the source of everything with human concepts, "For My thoughts are not your thoughts, neither are your ways My ways, says the Lord" (Isaiah 55:8). Albert Einstein was also aware of the limits of our understanding of the laws of nature: "[The scientist's] religious feeling takes the form of a rapturous amazement at the harmony of natural law, which reveals an intelligence of such superiority that, compared with it, all the systematic thinking and acting of human beings is an utterly insignificant reflection."[15]

We are incapable of grasping the essence of God, for He is the most primary entity. He is the most general, the most comprehensive, entity, from which everything is derived. As Maimonides states:

It is the most basic of basic principles and a support for wisdom to know that there is something [namely God] that existed before anything else did and that He created everything that there is. Everything in the skies, on the ground and in between exists only because of the fact that He created them. Let it be known that if the Creator did not exist then

---

15. *Ideas and Opinions*, p. 40

nothing else would, for nothing can exist independently of the Creator. Let it further be known that if everything ceased to exist, the Creator alone would exist and would not have ceased to exist like everything else had.[16]

The essence of God is beyond our comprehension, He is *transcendent*. One might say that when we arrive at God's existence through theoretical reasoning only, it does not have an impact on our lives. Human beings are not capable of understanding a *transcendent* God, and we cannot understand His relationship towards us or whether He is involved in worldly matters or not. Belief in the existence of God through intellectual reasoning alone cannot be the basis of any religion. Only when God reveals himself and intervenes in man's life does it change his life. So the question is this: Are there any scientific tools for studying divine revelations? The answer is straightforward: Science cannot contribute anything to the issue of divine revelation. By its very nature, science studies things that are found in large quantities, such as atoms and molecules, and recurring events, such as the four seasons. In contrast, every encounter between human beings is a one-off event that does not recur. If that is the case then clearly every encounter with the divine is a unique experience.

Many individuals have felt God's presence in a very profound way, but we, the Jewish people, have a collective memory of His revelations. We owe the essence of our peoplehood to our connection with God and His revelations, a connection documented in the ancient annals of history of the Jewish people. This book, the Bible, is a book of testimonies of numerous revelations that occurred to the nation, and to individuals within the nation, over a fairly long period of time. The Bible does not deal with proofs of the existence of God at all, but rather it tells of people's encounters with Him. This book, because of its content, has been preserved and passed on from generation to generation, with the utmost

---

16. *Mishne Torah, The Book of Knowledge, Fundamentals of Torah* 1:1-3

fidelity. The God of Israel is the God of Abraham, the God of Isaac and the God of Jacob. He is both a **transcendent** God and a **personal** God, with whom we can have a connection, and He is also a **normative** God, setting norms of behavior for us and commanding us to comply with them.

In Chapter One we discussed the uniqueness of man compared with all the other creatures. Now we will focus on man's most important attribute – his soul that is connected to God. Maimonides writes in his *Guide of the Perplexed*:

Now man possesses as his proprium something in him that is very strange as it is not found in anything else that exists under the sphere of the moon, namely, intellectual apprehension. In the exercise of this, no sense, no part of the body, none of the extremities are used; and therefore this apprehension was likened unto the apprehension of the deity, which does not require an instrument, although in reality it is not like the latter apprehension, but only appears so to the first stirrings of opinion. It was because of this something, I mean *because of the divine intellect conjoined with man*, that it is said of the latter that he is in the image of God and in His likeness... (*Guide of the Perplexed*, 1:1)

Elsewhere Maimonides explains that the connection between man and God is continuous, at least as a possibility, but man is given the option to strengthen or weaken this connection:

You have the choice: if you wish to strengthen and to fortify this bond, you can do so; if, however, you wish gradually to make it weaker and feebler until you cut it, you can also do that. (Ibid. 3:51)

The concept of the openness of man's soul to God is deeply rooted in the Jewish worldview. The Bible is full of events that testify to the connection between man and God, and man plays an active role in the creation of this connection – he must constantly direct all his thoughts to it: "I have set the Lord always before me; surely He is at my right hand, I shall not be moved." (Psalms 16:8). A connection with God, a desire to be close to Him and actions to realize the holiness in man's life give life meaning, a subject that we shall discuss in detail later on. But there is a different view that is common in secular thought, a view that holds that the goal of man is to be happy, where happiness is considered to be maximum personal pleasure. As we have explained, man is a far more complex and sophisticated creature than all other living things. Therefore he has many tools for the achievement of pleasure. Abraham Joshua Heschel quotes from the definition of *man* in the Encyclopedia Britannica: "Man is a seeker after the greatest degree of comfort for the least necessary expenditure of energy."[17] But he is therefore no different from an animal: "For that which befalls the sons of men befalls beasts; even one thing befalls them; as the one dies, so dies the other; yea, they have all one breath; so that man has no pre-eminence above a beast; for all is vanity." (Ecclesiastes 3:19)

Nevertheless, when we look closely at the phenomenon of man we see that he has a quality that clearly distinguishes him from animals, and that quality is *creativity*. He is able to create new things that did not exist previously. Of course man could also use this quality purely for his only selfish pleasure. Later we will bring a rational argument for the necessity of the openness of man's soul to God, and we will connect this openness with man's creativity. But it is important to emphasize that from the secular philosopher's point of view, when he truly studies the subject consistently, the phenomenon of creativity is the biggest mystery in the world. Popper writes:

I would even suggest that the greatest riddle of cosmology may well be neither the original big bang, nor the problem why there is something rather than nothing... but that the universe is, in a sense, creative: that it created life, and from it mind - our consciousness - which illuminates

---

17. A. J. Heschel, *Between God and Man*, p. 233

the universe, and which is creative in its turn...Einstein said something like this: "If there were not this internal illumination, the universe would merely be a rubbish heap."[18]

Now let us look at the phenomenon of man from a purely secular perspective, and let us try to understand why his creativity is a mystery. When a baby is born, he has many traits and propensities. As he develops he is capable of absorbing a large amount of knowledge from his environment, and thus his connection to the spiritual world of human culture grows and strengthens. This spiritual world contains science, technology, art, religion, philosophy and the like – everything that humankind has achieved up to that point. From a naturalistic perspective, one that is without God, other than man and his world of knowledge there is no spiritual entity which can provide additional knowledge on top of that which is found in man and humankind. From here it follows that each store of knowledge that a person possesses is composed of his personal knowledge and the knowledge that he can draw from the spiritual world of human culture.

If a person has never learnt or been taught French, for example, he will not know French. He cannot create the knowledge of the French language by himself. If this is so, then the question arises: If all the knowledge in the world is comprised of the personal knowledge of all human beings and the knowledge that has accumulated in human culture, where can new knowledge appear from? It is worth pointing out that the appearance of new knowledge is a creation. What distinguishes a creation? It is something which does not follow, either logically or scientifically, from something that already exists. For example, a new scientific theory does not follow from any old theory, and if this was not the case it would not be a new creation, but just a consequence of or an addition to the old theory. It is important to understand that anything that is new is not

---

18. Karl R. Popper and John C. Eccles, The Self and Its Brain, p. 61

inherent in something that already exists, otherwise it would not be new but would just be a logical result of the old thing and inherent in it. True creation is ex nihilo – something that does not come from anything that already exists in the world. In other words, the "creativity of nature" and the creativity of man are the greatest mysteries from the secular perspective. One needs the deep insight of Popper and Einstein to comprehend this, to grasp this wondrous aspect of reality amidst the routine. Indeed, according to the naturalistic worldview, which is devoid of God, the phenomenon of creativity in general, and the creativity of man in particular, is the "greatest riddle of cosmology".

When we realize that there are things which appear in our world *ex nihilo*, it leads to the conclusion that our world and each of our souls are not closed, complete entities, but are open to an external source. These things seem *ex nihilo* when we do not recognize the external factor. In fact, both the world and our souls are open to God, and therefore true creation is always connected to God. To illustrate this, I brought the following analogy in my book *Creation Ex Nihilo*:

Basically, the entire physical world is comprised of matter and light. Now, let us imagine that we know nothing about the existence of light. Then we will "see" strange things take place in the world of matter: matter is not conserved, here and there matter is created out of nothing, and it sometimes disappears. The world is no longer strange when light is added to the picture. Light can create matter and matter can disappear when an atom goes to a higher energy state with the emission of a photon. In this parable, matter represents our world and everything in it, including humanity and the human mind. Light is God.

The Torah teaches us that *new* knowledge, as compared with that which already exists, comes to us by divine providence. In the Torah portion Miketz, which is in the book of Genesis, Pharaoh has a dream: Seven fat cows emerge from the River Nile, followed by seven haggard and lean cows which proceed to eat the seven fat cows. He falls asleep again and has a second dream: Seven good, healthy ears of corn grow, followed by seven thin and bare ears of corn which then swallow the healthy ears. The Egyptian scholars did not manage to interpret Pharaoh's dreams, but his butler was reminded of a young Hebrew man, Joseph, who correctly interpreted his dream while they were together in prison. Pharaoh calls Joseph to him, who then proceeds to correctly interpret the dreams. His interpretation – that there would be seven years of plenty followed by seven years of famine – had important ramifications for the kingdom, for Joseph's life and for the entire Jewish nation. But we must understand that there was no way of arriving at that interpretation through simple logic. Joseph also understood this well. This was new knowledge which only God bestows on a person and humanity. The words that Joseph said to Pharaoh actually express the essence of the Jewish theory of knowledge: "And Joseph answered Pharaoh, saying: 'It is not in me; God will give Pharaoh an answer of peace.'" (Genesis 41:16) The meaning of this is clear: It is not I, Joseph, a human being, who is creating this new knowledge, but it is God who will answer.

Let us conclude by saying that man's soul is open to God, and new knowledge enters it by divine revelation. As we have already mentioned, this principle is firmly rooted in Judaism, it originated in the Torah and found its way to the philosophies of major Jewish thinkers. We cited Maimonides earlier, but Rabbi Judah Halevi also stressed the importance and necessity of divine revelation for the attainment of true knowledge. He believed that anything that man comes to know by way of logical deduction is not knowledge of the spiritual reality but an abstraction that is devoid of content, and it goes without saying that it has no certainty. According to Rabbi Judah Halevi, the prophet is different from the philosopher in that he has a metaphysical experience that is based on an unmediated feeling of spiritual entities.

Solomon Maimon, whose real name was actually Solomon Ben Yehoshua, was born in the middle of the eighteenth century in Lithuania. As a child he received a traditional education in Talmud, and was soon recognized as a prodigy. Solomon was especially influenced by the works of Maimonides, and out of reverence for him, adopted the name "Maimon" to become Solomon Maimon. Maimon had a keen interest in philosophy, and through various means he found his way to Immanuel Kant who recognized his analytical skills. The breakthrough that Maimon made in the philosophy of scientific cognition, when he essentially overcame Kant, came from his Jewish background, and in particular from the legacy of Maimonides.

Maimon believed that the assumption of the existence of a divine entity is a requirement of reason for cognition and thought. He maintained that every person is aware of his finiteness and of his being contingent. He is not the cause itself or the cause of his objects, nor does he receive his objects from an external, non-rational source. Hence, only another intellect, an absolute intellect, can be the source for itself and for its objects. Scientific cognition can be based only on the assumption that there is an infinite intellect about which there is no new knowledge. In contrast, new knowledge is gradually revealed to human beings, ad infinitum. At the end of his book Essay on Transcendental Philosophy, Maimon writes: "Our Talmudic sages... say: 'Torah scholars have no rest either in this world or in the world to come', and in their usual way, they concur with the quotation from Psalms (84:8) 'They go from strength to strength, every one of them appears before God in Zion.'"

The German philosopher Freidrich Wilhelm Joseph von Schelling (1775-1854) developed a philosophy of art that was greatly influenced by the kabbalistic teachings of the Zohar and the Ari (Yitzhak Luria).[19]

---

19. Moshe Schwartz discusses Schelling's relationship with Judaism in his book, *From Myth to Revelation*.

True, original art is not an imitation of sensory reality by the imagination. According to Schelling, art is the embodiment of ideal comprehension that expresses the truth of the higher spheres. The Self of the artist-creator connects deeply to the higher intellect, to God, who is the creator of the universe, and who renews it and sustains it. In this way, art is actually a divine revelation.

Leo Baeck (1873-1956) asked himself where the prophet's ability to elevate himself above the experience of his mundane, day-to-day life comes from. What are the tools with which a man made of flesh and blood can feel the presence of God? Baeck found the answers to these questions in the teachings of Rabbi Judah Halevi, and he updated it using Schelling's theory. According to Baeck, the prophetic sense is not super-human. It is a potential quality that is revealed in the stage of early childhood of every person. Most people lose it as they grow up, but there are some individuals who maintain and nurture it, and it can then raise them to a level of prophetic inspiration. Amongst the Jewish nation the prophetic sense has appeared to an especially great degree, both in scope and in intensity.

Isaac Breuer (1883-1946) believed that the Oral Torah is not derived logically from the Written Torah, but a continuation of the prophet's revelation at Sinai, as an absolute ideal legislation from it, and as an authoritative commentary that makes it applicable to every generation by its constant renewal by Jewish scholars. The Oral Torah explains and applies the Written Torah as part of a continuous process of divine revelation.

Gershom Scholem (1897-1982) believed that Judaism is unified by a form of religious consciousness, which transfers its vast content in a coherent sequence from an infinite source and its own conduits of inspiration. The concept of "*kabbalah*" (meaning "receiving") expresses this accurately. Hence Scholem's assertion that the Kabbalah is the kernel that both distinguishes and unites Jewish culture.

"Moses received the Torah from Sinai and passed it down to Joshua..." The term "passed it down" in this context emphasizes the rational aspect of the transmission from generation to generation, while the word "received" stresses the supernatural aspect of receiving the content that was given from the absolute source. The action of the transmission reveals the rational power of the established halakhic instruction, while the act of receiving (*kabbalah*) shows the openness to the super-human, the super-rational, which is in the renewing creation. And, of course, the Kabbalah is beyond the established pool of knowledge. The revelationary meaning of the Torah creation is expressed in the Kabbalah, and it is the Kabbalah that designates this word to the expression of the mystical foundation inherent in it. Scholem was aided by the philosophy of Schelling, for whom myth and mysticism, and in particular biblical myth and kabbalistic mysticism, held a central place in his overall philosophy.

But here we must express some reservations: It is not only the Kabbalah, but also the Oral Torah, as Rabbi Isaac Breuer pointed out, and in fact anything that contains new knowledge, is received as part of a continuous process of divine revelation.

According to Rabbi Avraham Yitzhak Hacohen Kook (1865-1935), everything that we know is originally anchored in prophecy, and only afterwards is it learned and the tool of man's wisdom is required. Prophecy produces a completely new creation. The prophet feels the flow of prophecy as it passes through the channels of his soul, and he is aware with complete certainty that his soul has a connection with the infinite divine.

One can see this trend clearly in the writings of Rabbi Kook. He views all of culture, in all its varied forms, as divine revelation:

The laws of life, laws of heaven and earth, shine with supreme light, light of greatness, light of vitality in all of existence in its highest form, wide and full, the light of everlasting life and source of all life. All the teachings, statutes, ideas, ethics, naturalness, orders and manners, wisdoms, songs and wills, the turbulence of life, movements of existence, its progress and grasp on the essence of being, all are but treasure houses filled with riches; the will that rises for our sake in his mighty power and the majesty of his lasting endurance in the foundation of his magnificence and the sublime desire of his glorious majesty, this will shall be revealed and visible in them in full brilliance. (Lights of Holiness, Vol. II, section 3)[20]

The short, incomplete selection above[21] reinforces the principle of revelation: *Man's soul is open to God, and new knowledge enters the soul as divine revelation* – a principle firmly rooted in Judaism. One should note that without this principle, the phenomenon of human creativity is regarded by the secular worldview as a mystery.

For secular thought, scientific cognition in general and creativity in particular, are a mystery for which there is no rational explanation, and this is a *flaw* in the fabric of secular thought. Furthermore, in this section (and in Chapter One) a picture that contradicts the common secular view has become clear to us. Man is not just a superior, advanced animal on the evolutionary ladder, but a creature that is capable of forming a connection with God. Every person has this quality, at least in potential if not actually. Despite the fact that this ability is realized only rarely over the course of a person's life, and only certain individuals are capable of realizing this potential in the form of a message intended for the masses, it is this quality that differentiates man from all other living creatures.

---

20. Translation from *Rav Avraham Itzhak HaCohen Kook: between rationalism and mysticism*, Binyamin Ish Shalom, 1993

21. In compiling this selection I was aided by Eliezer Schweid's *History of the Philosophy of the Jewish Religion in Modern Times.*

5. Reason, Logic and Philosophy

How do we get to know the world and everything in it? How reliable are the various tools that we use to understand the world? The answers to these questions and to others related to understanding the world are extremely important. Each of our worldviews, whether consciously or sub-consciously, is dependent on an understanding of the sources of our knowledge of the world. For example, many people – ordinary individuals and those who are considered intellectuals and experts alike – are convinced that science provides the answers to all existential questions, including understanding our place in the world and the meaning of our lives. We saw in Chapter Two, section 4 that in the "scientific" world – that is governed solely by the laws of nature – there is no place for man as a creature with free will and as someone who is capable of creating new things. Hence it was important for us to understand what the source of scientific knowledge is, and what the limitations of science are. We dealt with this subject in the earlier sections.

Now let us ask ourselves a general question: What tools do we have at our disposal for understanding the world and our place in it? In contrast to other creatures, man is endowed with reason, with intellect. Comprehension of the world means understanding its structure, its laws and its development, and understanding the meaning of our lives. These goals belong to the realms of science, religion and philosophy. We have already spoken about science – now let us take a look at the concept of philosophy. The Encyclopedia Britannica defines *philosophy* as: "the rational, methodical, and systematic consideration of those topics that are of greatest concern to humankind". In Webster's dictionary, philosophy is defined as "a search for the underlying causes and principles of reality", with the search not being carried out through observations, experiments and the analysis of theses, but through the use of logic. I also came across a definition of philosophy as a "critical contemplation of reality".

A clear distinction must be made between two things – philosophical problems and the ways to find solutions and answers to these problems. Philosophical problems may be real, but it is impossible to solve them using only reason. To explain what I mean I will need, first, to bring examples of philosophical problems and then to explain what logic is, and why it is impossible to solve philosophical problems by reason alone.

We came across philosophical topics above, and in fact most of the things that we have discussed are philosophical in nature: the problem of free will versus determinism; whether the world is governed solely by the laws of nature or there is room for the intervention of the wills of man and divine providence; whether matter is the source of all things or there is also a spiritual world. Questions and problems of this type do not belong to science, that is, there is no possibility of examining them through experience. Nonetheless, there are those who think that it is possible to solve everything using scientific tools, and if there are problems that science has not yet been able to solve, then sooner or later it will manage to solve them. In this chapter we have already spoken about science and its limitations, but it is clear that there are philosophical problems which do not belong to science. Science is involved in describing the laws of nature, but it is not capable of explaining why there is lawfulness and order in the world at all, and likewise, it cannot explain the uniformity of the laws of nature throughout the entire world. We have seen that from a secular perspective the structural uniformity of the universe resists a "deeper explanation" – it remains a mystery. Even though these problems are not scientific, they are of supreme importance in the life of man. Thus, from the recognition that free will exists comes the conclusion that man is responsible for his actions, while without it there could be no civilized society. Similarly, recognition of the existence of God has a vital effect on the behavior of man and society.

Now let us try to understand what logic is, why it must be used in order to describe reality, and what its limitations are. It is clear that in order to understand the world we must know how to infer conclusions regarding different aspects of reality, how to infer conclusions from premises. *The goal of logic is to infer true conclusions from true premises*, or in other words, logic is the means, the tool, for drawing true conclusions. When I use the word "proof", I am referring to proof according to the rules of logic. First, I shall bring a few examples of *logical inference, deduction and drawing correct conclusions*. The concept of *logic* was developed in ancient Greece, in particular in the work of Aristotle, as the art of reasoning and argument. So, let us take an example from the Greeks.

All people are mortal. Greeks are people. Therefore Greeks are mortal.

From the true premise that *All people are mortal*, the true conclusion is drawn that *Greeks are mortal*. It is important to note here that the correctness, or truth, of the conclusion derives from the fact that all Greeks are people, and from the valid premise that people are mortal. If we had been able to find just one Greek who was not a person, then the proof would not have been correct. The drawing of a conclusion, *deduction*, is valid only if a *counter-example* does not exist.

Here is an example of an erroneous deduction, because of the existence of a counter-example:

All people are mortal. Socrates is mortal. Therefore Socrates is a person.

Note: We have here a true premise – *all people are mortal*, and a true conclusion–*Socrates is a person* – but the inference is not correct, and this is because there is a counter-example. Let's say that Socrates is the name of a dog. Hence, from the inference it is derived that a dog is a person, and this is a wrong conclusion. This inference brings us both to a correct conclusion – the philosopher Socrates is a person – and to an incorrect conclusion – the dog Socrates is a person. Therefore this inference is not valid since using it can lead to incorrect conclusions.

We have determined that inference, a rule for drawing conclusions, is valid if and only if there is no counter-example that contradicts it or if it is possible to show that this example does not exist. The two examples brought above are simple ones. Mathematics provides us with more complex examples for drawing conclusions. At the foundation of geometry lie a few basic premises, called *axioms*. From these axioms, many conclusions are inferred using logic – these are *theorems*. For example, *the angles in any triangle add up to 180°*, or, *in an equilateral triangle all the angles are equal*. Arithmetic also provides countless inferences that are derived from particular premises.

Logic deals with the analysis of drawing correct conclusions from certain premises, which are also considered correct. "Considered" – this is where the connection to reality comes in. What do I mean? From a purely mathematical perspective, the correctness, or truthfulness, of the axioms is guaranteed by the very *declaration* that they are true. Sounds strange? Not really. In fact, mathematical claims are always *conditional*: if the axioms are true, then it is possible to prove that a particular inference is also true. However, gaining a *true description* of reality, and aspiring to draw conclusions about it are another matter entirely. Hence, we must determine the relationship between the premises of logic or mathematics and the facts of reality. In fact, mathematics provides us with a *language* for describing reality, a subject we discussed in Chapter Two, section 1.

What is important to us at this point is to understand the limitations of logical proofs. Basically, logical proof does not create anything new; it simply brings to light that which is already inherent in a fundamental premise. Take a look at the example discussed above:

All people are mortal. Greeks are people. Therefore Greeks are mortal.

Here the premise *All people are mortal* is talking about *all* people, including Greeks, Romans, Jews, Persians etc. This means that Greeks are latently included in the premise that *All people are mortal.* The conclusion, *Therefore Greeks are mortal,* only highlights something that already exists in the premise. Therefore, on the one hand, logical proof is a solid, secure tool, but on the other hand, it does not actually produce anything new.

However, philosophy is not mathematics. Mathematics can play games – what would the conclusions from these and other premises be? – without questioning the truth of those premises. Philosophy, on the other hand, claims to describe, explain and understand reality, the real world, and not imaginary worlds like those of mathematics. Therefore, philosophy is not entitled to "declare" the correctness of its premises. Human reason and logic are not capable of proving the correctness of the foundations of one philosophical approach or another.

Since the time of the Ancient Greeks numerous philosophies have arisen. The history of human thought is full of different philosophies with different premises, and there is no way of determining, using philosophical tools and reason, the truth or otherwise of any premise of any philosophical doctrine. We have seen that it is impossible, using logic alone, to answer the questions such as whether man has free will, whether our world is deterministic or non-deterministic, whether matter is the source of all things or whether the spirit has an independent existence. It is impossible to prove or deny these statements either by logic or by experience, but nonetheless, one cannot say that there is no benefit to philosophical activity. Critical observation of reality brings up many questions and issues which are not apparent in our day-to-day lives and thinking.

Greek philosophy defined a number of general philosophical questions, the first of which was: What is the source of all that exists? This question is dealt with by the field of philosophy called metaphysics. The second question is: Does absolute knowledge exist? An entire field of philosophy, epistemology, deals with the way in which knowledge of the world is achieved and the source of our knowledge. The field of ethics tackles

The Imaginary Worlds of Mathematics

Mathematics started to develop in a systematic way in Ancient Greece. Euclid, a Greek mathematician who lived in Alexandria, Egypt in the third and fourth century BCE, wrote the *Elements*, a treatise of thirteen books in which he systematically analyzed the results of mathematical research and knowledge that had accumulated up to that period. He laid the foundations of the geometry that bears his name: Euclidean geometry, which is based on a number of premises – axioms. From these axioms, various theorems can be logically derived.

Until the nineteenth century, the naïve opinion that axioms do not need to be proved as they are self-evident was commonly held. However, there was one axiom – the parallel postulate – the fifth of the axioms of geometry in Euclid's book, which did not seem self-evident. For centuries, mathematicians tried to prove that this axiom could be derived from the other axioms, namely that it is not an axiom but a theorem. These efforts were in vain until a major breakthrough was made at the start of the nineteenth century. First was Gauss, who thought that the parallel postulate could be replaced with another axiom, thereby arriving at a different geometry from Euclidean geometry but one that is equally valid. After Gauss, the Russian mathematician Nikolai Lobachevsky and the Hungarian army officer Janos Bolyai came up with the same idea. Bernhard Riemann, a student of Gauss's, established an infinite group of non-Euclidean geometries called Riemannian geometries.

Hence there is an infinite number of imaginary mathematical worlds, and, from a mathematical perspective, one cannot have preference for any one over another. Mathematics cannot decide which of these worlds is closer to the real world in which we live – this is a matter for physics. Indeed, Albert Einstein discovered in his general theory of relativity a connection between the geometry of space and time and the physical characteristics of the world.

questions related to morality and the meaning of human life. There are other fields, but the nature of the questions with which philosophy deals is already clear. It is important to ask questions, and that is what philosophy excels in, but it is impossible to give answers using philosophical tools, that is, through logic alone. The fact that there are many philosophical approaches that give different answers to the same questions is testament to this point. Just as different mathematical axioms lead to different mathematical structures, the premises of different philosophies lead to different conclusions about the structure of the world. The difference is that modern mathematics does not claim to show or prove the truth of its axioms, while every philosopher is certain of the correctness of his approach. But when a person is offered different answers to the same question, he is likely to come to the conclusion that philosophy does not have the answers to his existential questions.

I once heard a lecture at Tel Aviv University about Maimonides' *Guide of the Perplexed*. The lecturer wanted to explain that Maimonides tried to conceal, using certain tools, his true opinion of divine providence, and, turning to his students with an all-knowing grin, said, "Of course you understand that from a philosophical perspective, there can be no divine providence!" I mention this incident, so as to emphasize that there is no such thing as "from a philosophical perspective" – philosophy does not have the power to prove or refute the existence of divine providence.

If this is the case, then one can ask the following: What is Jewish philosophy? What have generations of Jewish philosophers been doing? We have seen that philosophy itself does not create its premises but offers them as eternal truths that do not require any proof. In contrast, one might expect that Jewish philosophy would draw its premises from the Bible, but this is just wishful thinking. In fact, different Jewish philosophers, in addition to relying on biblical sources, have also used sources of philosophy that were foreign to the spirit of Jewish thought.

It is worth mentioning that most of the Jewish philosophers in medieval times had a problem reconciling Jewish thought with the philosophies of Plato and Aristotle. "The most central concepts of medieval Jewish philosophy are rooted in ancient Greek and medieval Arabic thought and are not of Jewish origin at all. It is impossible to reconstruct a unique Jewish world perspective out of alien material."[22] There were some thinkers at the time who understood this, such as Rabbi Judah Halevi, who, in his book, *The Kuzari*, displayed strong reservations about using philosophy as a source of existential truth for the life of man. Unfortunately, also nowadays, there is a tendency to rely on sources that are foreign to Judaism. Only in modern times have many thinkers, both Jewish and non-Jewish, grappled with the philosophy of Kant, and tried to reconcile it with Judaism. Rabbi Soloveitchik writes: "Since the time of the great medieval philosophers, Jewish philosophical thought has expressed itself... upon premises, which were more non-Jewish than Jewish. The most characteristic example is to be found in Hermann Cohen's *philosophy of religion*... There are many truths in his interpretation, but the main trends are idealistic Kantian and not Jewish."[23] The Sages expressed a similar view: "If a person tells you there is wisdom among the nations of the world, believe him. If a person tells you there is Torah among the nations of the world, do not believe him." (Eichah Rabbah, 2:13)

Philosophy does not create new truths. Every philosophical doctrine is based on its own premises, and there is no, and nor can there be any, proof of their validity. It is impossible to prove the correctness of the premises of a particular philosophical doctrine, but nevertheless, from a critical examination of reality, one can arrive at certain logical conclusions. We saw in the first section that David Hume proved that it is impossible to derive any theory logically from the data of an experiment. In Chapter Four, section 6 we will bring a number of proofs for the inability of the

---

22. Rabbi J.B. Soloveitchik, *The Halakhic Mind*, p. 100

23. Ibid., p. 101

evolutionary process – in a world that is closed to God – to lead to the creation of man. What all these examples have in common is that they are negative claims that deny something. But we shall discuss this further in Chapter Four, section 6.

What is the lesson that we can learn from this section for our continuing discussion on secularism? The lesson is simple: A secular thinker is not entitled to claim that his approach is correct because it is based on a particular philosophical approach. This is not a proof of the validity of his view, since there is no criterion in our world that can distinguish between different philosophies and can verify one of them. Only a source external to the world can get to the truth. In other words, the truth can only be attained as a divine revelation; however, there is no such thing in the secular vocabulary.

6. Conclusion: The Place of Science in Knowledge of the World

"Science is very successful in its limited field of problems; but the great problems, the *mysterium tremendum*, in the existence of everything we know, this is not accountable for in any scientific manner."

(K.R. Popper and J.C. Eccles, *The Self and Its Brain*, p. 564)

Now we can summarize our understanding of the place of science in the overall picture of the world in which we live. The view common amongst both laymen and those who regard themselves, rightly or wrongly, as intellectuals and experts is that science is capable of describing everything in the world, including human beings, and the development of the world itself. Science develops and over the course of time new horizons open up. Things that, yesterday, were a mystery, today science provides a satisfactory explanation for them. In the past, physics was not able to explain electromagnetic phenomena, and then along came the electromagnetic field theory and explained them. Of course modern physics is not yet a perfect science – there are still gaps. There is still no plausible theory that combines quantum theory and the general theory of relativity, which is the modern theory of gravity. But it is reasonable to assume that in the future such a theory will appear.

Science is constantly developing and closing the gaps within it. In contrast, religion focuses on things that science has not yet explained – on the "gaps" of science. Science develops, closes its "gaps", and at the same time the realm of science shrinks. That which is not understood today and appears to be a miracle and a mystery, will receive a scientific explanation tomorrow. People that hold this worldview use the expression "God of the Gaps". This God only exists because of people's ignorance: *necessary ignorance*, since science has not yet managed to solve all the problems, and *illiterate ignorance* which derives from a lack of knowledge of those issues that science has actually succeeded in explaining thus far.

It is important to understand that this kind of view is very commonly held these days, and can be called "scientific atheism" – atheism that is based, as it were, on the achievements of science. We have already seen, and we shall see in due course, the utter unreasonable of the atheist view that seeks its legitimacy in the achievements of science.

Hence, let us summarize what it is that characterizes science and distinguishes it from other enterprises of human intellect, such as mathematics and philosophy. Scientific theories are distinguished by the fact that they can all be tested through experiments and observations. A particular scientific theory can be corroborated by experiments, but it is impossible to verify it, that is, to prove that it is true. In contrast, a necessary feature of a scientific theory is that in principle it is possible to refute it by further experiments. A hypothesis that is impossible to corroborate or refute is not a scientific hypothesis. To call something "not scientific" is not a derogatory term for a hypothesis or entity that cannot be tested by experiment – it is also impossible to corroborate or refute the existence of free will by any experiment, but one cannot denounce those who believe in free will and say that they are ignoramuses who are not taking into account the achievements of science, just as one cannot condemn those who do not believe in free will.

It is important to understand that a description of reality is not limited to scientific achievements. Science only describes a particular aspect of reality, that can be tested by experiment. Events and objects that are unique cannot be described using scientific tools, since a scientific theory, by its very nature, deals with things that exist in multiple copies and recurring events. It is specifically the unique things and events that are, from a certain perspective, the most important to us, even though they cannot be the subject of scientific study. Creations, in various fields, are unique things, and such things cannot be the subject of scientific study. And my own Self, the unique element in me and in each of us, cannot be the subject of scientific study. So it seems that it is the most important things do not belong to science.

Metaphysical statements, such as the determinism or non-determinism of the world, causality in natural processes and belief in free will cannot be tested by experiments and cannot be refuted by either science or logic. And the argument that everything in the world belongs to science and can be explained by science is not a scientific argument – it is a metaphysical one, and hence it cannot be tested using scientific tools or through logical reasoning. Furthermore, the existence of any scientific theories and of science in general is a matter of belief. It is impossible to prove, either by logic or experience, that a particular scientific theory, which has managed to explain numerous phenomena up until now, will also succeed in explaining future phenomena. This was the essence of David Hume's discovery, that we discussed above. The assumption that there is lawfulness in the world and that it can be understood is in fact one of the beliefs of Judaism and other religions. Scientific theories are not proven, they are all only hypotheses, and also the assumption that science will continue to describe any phenomena in the future is nothing but a belief.

What is the answer to the "God of the Gaps" argument, that as science develops it describes more and more phenomena and shrinks the realm of religion? From the discussion above it follows that there are many subjects that, by their nature, do not belong to science and cannot be the subject of any scientific study. The claim that everything belongs to science and hence that sooner or later all the gaps will be closed, that everything that is not understood today will be explained scientifically tomorrow, is absolutely not a scientific claim. Therefore, in the following chapters, which discuss the history of the world, we will distinguish between the issues of the development of the world that belong to science and those that, cannot. We have already seen, and we shall see later on, that the secular, naturalist, godless view is full of *gaps* which it is incapable of closing. It is not the *God of the gaps*, but *secularism with gaps*!

There is another aspect to the "gaps" in the secular approach. The secular view presumes to explain all the processes of the world using scientific tools. However, what characterizes science is its desire for objectivity, meaning, its independence of a human factor. A person carrying out an experiment tries to take particular care to prevent the influence of any person on the results. Hence the results of the scientific study are not dependent on the effect of the human spirit on them. Natural science thereby removes man's spirit from its field of operation. However, the human spirit is not the only spirit that operates in the world, and even if it is possible to ignore the human spirit, it is impossible to ignore the divine spirit and not to be dependent on it. It is true that the secular premise is that the divine spirit that intervenes in earthly matters does not exist, but this does not mean that it does not exist in reality. In Chapter Two, section 2 we brought an analogy of a car driven by a person. An external observer watching the movement of the car traveling at a fixed speed on a straight road might think that it is only moving according to the laws of physics, whereas the fact is that the driver is in charge of the movement of the car at every moment. Similarly, we are liable to mistakenly think that the world develops solely in accordance with the laws of nature, without God's providence, while in fact divine providence is constantly operating and the laws of nature are simply one of its tools. A scientific description of different processes is based on the premise of the non dependence of these processes on any spirit. But, in fact, according to our belief, providence exists and is involved in all processes. Hence it is no wonder that the secular account contains things that cannot be explained – it has *gaps*.

CHAPTER FOUR: THE CREATION OF THE WORLD AND ITS DEVELOPMENT

1. The Creation of the World, and the Development of the Inanimate World

The concept of the creation of the world is one of the most fundamental principles of the Bible, and is a basis for the new worldview that the Bible brought to the world. It is important to stress that, just like the question of whether God exists, the concept of the creation of the world belongs to the realm of metaphysics – it is not a matter of science. Sometimes people mistakenly confuse the two fields.

Thus, in the nineteenth century, people thought that the Bible's version contradicted the scientific data, since according to the scientific view at that time the world had always existed. However, this was not actually a scientific view but rather a metaphysical one. Meanwhile, in the twentieth century, people began to search for corroboration of the concept of creation in modern physics. There are those who think that the Big Bang Theory describes the act of creation. However, even in the best case scenario, the Big Bang Theory can only describe the expansion of the world after the creation, not creation itself. The creation of the world does not belong to the realm of science. After the world has been created, physics can investigate its laws. But the creation of the world also includes the creation of its laws and of time and space, concepts that belong to a world that has already been created. The creation of the world itself must therefore be examined on a metaphysical level.

We shall expand a little more on the metaphysical, non-scientific, nature of the concepts of the creation of the world or the eternity of the world, since this is one of the key areas of conflict between the different views of the nature of the world. As we have mentioned, there are two possibilities regarding when the world came into existence. The traditional materialist assumption is that *materia* is eternal – matter has always existed. Therefore, the world, which itself is fundamentally a material entity, is also eternal. The world was not created; it has always existed. In contrast, the creation of the world and its finite age are at the basis of the biblical approach.

It is easy to understand that the eternity of the world is not a scientific assumption but a metaphysical one, since it is impossible to prove or refute this assumption using any scientific tools. There is no experiment that can corroborate the eternal nature of the world, nor is there one that can disprove it. An experiment that proves that a particular event happened only a certain amount of time ago does not contradict the fact that another event could have happened prior to it, and so on into infinity. One way or another, it is clear that no experiment can prove or corroborate the infinite age of the universe.

It is clear that this reasoning leads to the conclusion that also the idea that the world was created, that the world has a finite age, cannot be proven or disproved using scientific tools. But it is a fairly widely held view that the Big Bang Theory provides a scientific explanation for the creation of the world, just as the theory of evolution provides a scientific explanation for the creation of life and its development. We shall discuss this latter statement in due course. For now, we shall ask ourselves whether it is possible, in principle, to describe the event of the creation of the world using scientific tools. We have explained that a unique event – and the creation of the world is, without a doubt, such an event – does not belong to the realm of science and science cannot describe it. But there is a crucial difference between all the events that happen in the world, including the unique ones, and the creation of the world itself. All the other events take place in a world in which the laws of nature operate, while the creation of the world includes the creation of those very laws, the creation of time and space. To provide a scientific explanation means to explain and describe something using the existing laws of time and space. So, when we are talking about the creation of the world, this is not something that has simply not yet been explained by science, and which we can be certain that, sooner or later, will be explained as science develops. It is not a "gap" or a deficiency in the scientific account, which will be filled in the course of time! We need to get away from the irrational belief that everything in the world, including the creation of the world itself, can be explained and described by science. The creation of the world is a special event, the uniqueness of which is also expressed in the *creation* of the laws of nature, and therefore it does not belong to science. It should be noted that the very idea of the creation of the world is an indication of the openness of the world – something has been created *ex nihilo*, that is, there is something that is external to the world that determines the law and order within it.

Nevertheless, it is interesting to know what science says about the time close to the creation of the world, since even in the period of time immediately following the creation of the world the laws of nature were already created, and hence, in principle, it could have a scientific account. The concept of a world that was concentrated in one point and expands over time is related to Einstein's general theory of relativity. The solution of the "Big Bang" – that the world started its existence in one point – derives from Einstein's equations. It would seem that, in contrast to what we have said, the theory of relativity describes the development of the world including the starting point, the point of creation. But in fact, in the time period close to this starting point the theory of relativity is not applicable, and a more general theory is needed that also takes into account quantum phenomena. However, a theory of quantum relativity

– a consistent theory of quantum gravitation – still does not exist[1]. In contrast, all the attempts to take into account quantum phenomena in the period immediately following the creation of the world lead to the conclusion that the world also existed prior to the Big Bang – creation from something, as opposed to creation *ex nihilo*. In fact it could not be otherwise. Any scientific description, by its very nature, starts from the assumption that the scientific laws have always existed, both before and after creation, which is another way of expressing the conclusion that the act of the creation of the world does not belong to science at all. To scientifically explain something means to use the existing laws, but science is not capable of describing a borderline situation in which at one moment there are no laws and the next moment they have been created[2].

After the world was created it began to develop. In principle, this development could be the subject of scientific study. And that is what modern science tells us about the development of the world – the Big Bang scenario. In the beginning, fifteen billion years ago, the universe was in a very dense state (according to the theory of relativity, in one point), and from that time it began to expand and spread out. A billion years later the first stars and galaxies began to form. Around ten billion years after the Big Bang our solar system, containing our world, was formed. At a certain stage, approximately three-and-a half billion years ago, life was formed on Earth.

---

1. But nevertheless we can ask: How can it be that the theory of relativity, even if it is impossible to use it immediately following the creation of the world, also includes within it the point of creation, in contrast to what was stated above? To answer this question I shall quote Roger Penrose, an eminent scientist and an expert on singular points in the general theory of relativity: "... but *space-time singularities* are regions where our understanding of physics has reached its limits." (*The Emperor's New Mind*, p. 446)

2. Our concepts are not capable of describing the creation of the world. If it were written: "In the beginning there were no laws, and then they were created" we would be compelled at this point to introduce the dimension of time, which did not exist prior to the creation of the world but was created with it.

I said that in principle it is possible to describe the development of the world using scientific tools, but there is a problem. In general, science is not able to describe a one-off, unique event, and both the creation of the world and its development are such events. There is only one world (talk of multiple worlds belongs only to the field of metaphysics), and development is like the historical process, namely, it is a chain of interconnected events. One can imagine a situation where all the events in the chain are connected to each other by an unequivocal causal connection – *deterministic* development. Generally speaking, in historical development, unequivocal physical causation only applies in a limited domain, while it is the choices and decisions of human beings, important statesmen and ordinary citizens alike, that are likely to influence the course of human history. Thus, randomness also plays a vital role in the case of the development of life on Earth – the evolution of life – and we shall discuss further in due course.

Now we shall focus on the development of the inanimate world, before the appearance of life and man (or in places where they are not found). In these places man's spirit does not affect the development of the world, and in order to test whether science can describe it we shall, for a moment, ignore providence. Thus the laws of nature are the only factor that determines the development of the inanimate world. The question that we will try to answer is: Is a scientific description of the development of the inanimate world possible? This is a question that we will also ask ourselves in connection to other stages of development – the evolutionary stage and the historical stage – whether it is possible to describe them scientifically. This will all be discussed later. For the time being we will concentrate on the inanimate stage. If a scientific description is possible, then physics, at the foundation of which lies quantum theory, is the appropriate science for such a description. In quantum physics, random processes play a crucial role, but nonetheless, large blocks of matter which are themselves made up of quantum particles obey the classical deterministic laws which unequivocally determine their development, to a very close approximation. We assume that one can ignore the effect of random, quantum processes on the movements of the blocks of matter. But as we shall soon see, this is not always the case.

Therefore, we will assume that a certain stage in the development of the world after the Big Bang happens *deterministically*, according to deterministic laws that determine in advance the development of the inanimate world. Here we can use Popper's theory of scientific cognition (Chapter Three, section 2) to determine whether it is possible to use scientific tools in a description of this stage. Thus we assume that at the stage from the Big Bang until the formation of life, the development of the world can be described (deterministically) using the general theory of relativity and other laws of physics. Therefore all astrophysical information can corroborate or refute the hypothesis, and as long as it has not been refuted, it can serve as a scientific theory. If and when it is refuted by new experimental data, we will need to find a new hypothesis to replace the old one.

In fact, in the Big Bang scenario we use the laws of physics to describe the development of our one-of-a-kind universe, and we are able to make a certain amount of progress in describing the development of the world. Generally speaking, according to quantum theory there is no, scientific description of the development of a single object, such as our world and nor can there be any. But we will discuss this further later on. In the period of the development of the inanimate world it is hard for us to convincingly identify clear signs of divine providence, other than the monumental event of the creation of the world itself and the creation of the laws of nature, space and time. What we do know from scientific theories is that the formation of the stars and galaxies is compatible with the laws of physics. Perhaps the action of providence here is limited mainly to the operation of the laws of nature themselves.

We shall continue our discussion on secular thought, its

flaws and holes, at the end of the next section, which deals with the laws of nature and their creation.

2. The Creation of the Laws of Nature – the Anthropic Principle

According to scientific estimates, approximately ten billion years after the Big Bang our solar system was created, and within it, Planet Earth. Three-and-a-half billion years ago life was formed on Earth, and at a certain point man was created. An interesting question arises from the concept of the creation of the world: What should the laws that were created together with the world be like? We can suppose or imagine an assortment, an ensemble, of possible laws, from which the laws of nature that we are familiar with today were "chosen". We can also imagine other worlds with other systems of laws. The laws of physics are expressed using mathematical equations, which include parameters, constants, fixed universal quantities, such as the charges and masses of electrons and protons. The laws in the "other worlds" could be different from those in our world in the values of these fixed quantities, for example.

In short, it is possible to imagine laws of nature other than those that operate in our world. Therefore, it is interesting to analyze what worlds with other laws could be like. And what emerges from such an analysis? In worlds, imaginary or real, with laws of nature that differ even slightly from those in our world, the existence of animals and human beings would be impossible. Our world was created adjusted and fine-tuned to life on Earth. In other words, the world was designed in the subtlest of ways for the creation of life in general, and for the creation of the life of man in particular. And if there is a *design*, then there must be a *designer*.

When it became clear to scientists that the laws of nature are so precisely suited to the formation of life on Earth, the question arose of how this can be explained. The simplest explanation is to assume the existence of a designer. But the scientist, in general, seeks answers that do not involve a power outside of the realm of science. In other words, the scientist wants to explain everything using scientific tools. But the question regarding the creation of the laws of nature, just like the question of why these laws rather than any other laws exist, does not belong to the realm of science. These questions are external to science – they are metaphysical questions. But what has happened? The scientist, under the veil of scientific analysis, instead of recognizing the fact that he is dabbling purely in metaphysics and that he has ceased to act as a scientist, comes up with a theory, a metaphysical hypothesis, and thus attempts to "explain" the suitability of the laws of nature for the formation of life.

What are we talking about here? We are talking about the metaphysical hypothesis that, apart from our world, there is an infinite number of worlds with their own laws of nature. These laws of nature are distributed among the worlds on a completely random basis, from a series of different kinds of laws of nature with different universal physical constants. The "explanation" is as follows: Out of an infinite number of different worlds with different laws, there is also a world, one or more, whose laws are compatible with the existence of life, and clearly it is in a world of this kind that we, human beings, live. In other worlds the laws of nature are not suitable for the formation of life, and therefore creatures like us cannot exist there. This is called the "Weak Anthropic Principle". This is in contrast to the "Strong Anthropic Principle", which states that the laws of nature were created for the purpose of the formation of man. But it is clear that the hypothesis regarding the existence of many worlds is a metaphysical hypothesis, since there is no interaction, no reciprocal relationship, between our world and these other worlds. (And if there is any interaction between the worlds, then they are not different worlds, but simply different parts of the same world.) And the assumption regarding the difference in laws between the different worlds is an unmistakably metaphysical one. Hence, this explanation is also not scientific but rather a metaphysical one, a matter of belief.

As we have said, the anthropic principle does not give a proof for the existence of the creator-designer – neither a logical nor a scientific proof. There are many things in the world, including the existence of the world itself, for which we have no proof, but this does not prevent us from believing them wholeheartedly. A sane person has absolutely no doubt about the existence of our world, and even those who claim that they do not believe in free will conduct their daily lives with the sense of responsibility that derives from the existence of free will.

The anthropic principle does not prove the existence of the creator, but on the other hand, it cannot be ignored. It adds a layer to the foundations of belief in God. It is worth pointing out that the possibility of explaining, without the existence of a designer, the fact that the laws of nature are so precisely attuned to the formation of life on Earth is dependent on the assumption that there are worlds other than our world with different laws. If such worlds really existed then it would be possible to believe that we could explain why we live in a world with laws that are perfectly suited to the formation of life – human beings were not created in other worlds. But, as we have said, there is no scientific proof of the existence of other worlds. Therefore, the anthropic principle – the compatibility of the laws of nature with life – remains a mystery, a *gap* in the fabric of secular thought. The possibility that in the future science will prove the existence of other worlds is problematic, since such a scientific theory will need to be tested by experiment.

When we discuss the anthropic principle – whether the compatibility of the laws of nature with life means that there is a designer – we must take into account (see Chapter Two, section 1) that there is no scientific proof, and nor can there be, for the existence of the laws of nature. The more meaningful question is how the laws of nature can exist at all without a creator who created them. Secular thought does not answer this question. In Jewish thought, which recognizes a creator and the creation of the world, the existence of law and order in the world does not present a problem. It is also clear that the laws of nature must fulfill certain conditions, so that they can enable the appearance of man at a certain stage of its development. Furthermore, the laws of nature must be compatible with man's free will (See Chapter Two, section 6).

3. The Theory of Evolution – Science or Metaphysics?

Now we shall begin our discussion of the era of life in the development of the world. Rightly or wrongly, Darwin's theory of evolution is considered to be the most convincing theory for the secular, naturalist viewpoint, which sees nature as the source of everything, including the most complex and sophisticated creature of all – man. We must therefore clarify what Darwin's theory of evolution is, whether it is a scientific theory or simply a belief that is based on neither logic nor experience. In other words, we must clarify whether there are scientific arguments for the secular view that nature itself produces a diverse collection of creatures, with man at the top. In Chapter Three, section 4 we cited Karl Popper who phrases the question thus:

I would even suggest that the greatest riddle of cosmology may well be neither the original big bang, nor the problem why there is something rather than nothing… but that the universe is, in a sense, creative: that it created life, and from it mind - our consciousness - which illuminates the universe, and which is creative in its turn…

One way or another, the attribution of creativity to nature or to the world presents a riddle and mystery for the secular worldview. But not everyone thinks this way. The common notion, as we have mentioned, is that a scientific theory exists that can explain the formation and development of life on Earth using scientific tools, and hence can also explain the appearance of man. According to this view, Darwin's theory of evolution, which has been amended by the more recent discoveries in the field of biology, is a scientific theory that scientifically explains the development of life and the appearance of man on Earth. It should also be noted that even if a scientific theory for the formation of life and man did exist – it does not, and could not exist, as we shall see later – the secular view, which claims that there is a scientific explanation for all of reality, would not be vindicated. The creation of the laws that are fine-tuned to the formation of life – for these things, by their very nature, as for other things, there is not and nor can there be a scientific explanation. Nonetheless, from a psychological perspective, one can understand why the possibility of explaining the development of life scientifically weighs so heavily on people's minds. If there is a scientific explanation for a marvel as great as the appearance of man, then it is possible to hope that sooner or later a scientific explanation will be found for all the wonders and mysteries in the world. But this is a false hope, since, as we have explained several times, there are mysteries which do not belong to the realm of science at all.

Now we will try to understand what the evolution of life is, what Darwin's theory, which presumes to explain evolution, states, and why it is not a scientific theory but is a kind of metaphysical belief, which cannot be tested by experiment and cannot be proven (or refuted) by logic. According to modern scientific estimates, 3,500,000,000 years ago something new was formed on Earth that was nothing like anything that had existed there previously. The era of life began. Scientists believe that every living thing developed from one very simple, miniscule creature. Currently there are more than 2,000,000 different species in the world. They differ enormously from one another in terms of size, shape and life expectancy. But what is remarkable is that every living thing – all animals, from the simplest creatures to human beings, and even all plants – trees, flowers and weeds – are all built in the same way. One could say that living organisms are all highly complex and delicate "mechanisms", and what unites them all is their genetic material. From the simplest bacteria to humans we find the same genetic material – DNA – a large, long molecule, a chain of units, which only in its length (and in the text included in it) does man differ from the rest of the living creatures.

A living entity has an amazing quality that differentiates it from an inanimate object – it reproduces, it makes copies of itself and produces new living entities. It is the genetic material of the biological organism that is "responsible" for passing on the qualities of the organism to its offspring, and that preserves its identity for future generations, but it does not do this in an absolute way. One can identify tiny changes between the generations as well as between different individuals in the same species. A particular bacterium produces bacteria that are almost identical to it. Why "almost"? Why is the transfer from one generation to the next not absolute, and what causes it? The organism's genetic mechanism, which is found in its DNA, precisely copies all of its traits for its offspring, as long as the transfer takes place without any external intervention. However, it is impossible to entirely ignore the effect of the environment, even if it is fairly minimal at each stage of the organism's reproduction. In general, one can say that the genetic material contains detailed instructions for the building of the offspring's bodies. The incredible thing is that these instructions are written in a text whose letters are made up of molecules. When cosmic particles collide with the genetic material, they can cause changes, generally minimal ones, in the text of the genetic instructions. In most cases these changes, which are called mutations, are damaging and have a negative effect. But there are also some mutations that improve the genetic text, and lead to better adaptation to the environment, for example to an increased reproduction rate. Individuals whose genetic mutations are more positive end up surviving and reproducing, while those with less successful heredity either do not reproduce at all or do so at a reduced rate.

This mechanism of adaptation to the environment is called *natural selection*. In 1859, Charles Darwin, in his book, *On the Origin of Species*, proposed the natural selection mechanism, which he believed explains the process of the evolution of life. (In Darwin's time, people were not aware of the details of the heredity mechanism that we know today.)

We will summarize here the concept of the natural selection mechanism. It contains three elements: *heredity, mutations,* and *natural selection*. Mutations are random changes, which are caused by radioactive materials or cosmic particles. Mutations are responsible for genetic changes, that is, for errors in the genetic mechanism. Biology has come a very long way since Darwin's day, and now we know a lot about the physics and chemistry of the genetic mechanism, and we are able to decipher man's genetic code. However, the basic mechanism of *natural selection* is still considered the basis for understanding evolutionary change.

The natural selection mechanism is a vital tool for understanding countless biological phenomena. For example, we can explain and understand the adaptation of bacteria to certain antibiotics such as penicillin through the mechanism of natural selection. Penicillin destroys the majority of bacteria. However, a very tiny minority of bacteria, which came about as a result of mutations, are able to resist penicillin. These bacteria will pass on this quality to their offspring, and thus the penicillin-resistant bacteria will multiply.

The remarkable achievement of biology in the last century is the understanding that every living thing is made up of the same genetic material, which is the most conservative element of the organism. The genetic material determines the majority of the organism's *physical* attributes. A complete living organism develops from a seed ("Whence you came? From a putrid drop..." Ethics of the Fathers, 3:1), with all the instructions necessary for its development included in its genetic material.

Now that we have a basic understanding of the natural selection mechanism, we are ready to discuss Darwin's idea that this mechanism explains the evolution of life. It is important to distinguish between two different concepts: the *theory of evolution*, based on the adaptation mechanism of natural selection and the *fact of evolution*, namely the development of the profusion of life on Earth, which began from primitive organisms and gradually developed over time into self-conscious beings. Confusing these two concepts can lead to serious misunderstandings. We must also differentiate between the adaptation mechanism of *natural selection*, and the *theory of evolution*, since a successful explanation of any phenomenon of adaptation by the mechanism of natural selection is sometimes, mistakenly, understood as a corroboration of the "theory of evolution".

The fact of evolution is based not on one theory or another, but on *paleontological* data, on the gamut of *fossilized* remains of living things from different periods. We should note that even up until the present day, scientists argue about the essence of the idea of gradual evolution as a cause of the formation of new species. Eldridge and Gould explain the absence of intermediate fossil sequences by asserting that development is not gradual. They suggest that new species developed over the course of a few thousand years (a minuscule moment in geological terms) after which there were no changes for millions of years. They termed this kind of development "*punctuated equilibrium*".

We may ask ourselves the following question: What kind of certainty can we attribute to the possible explanation of the development of life on Earth? Throughout this book we have seen countless times that we cannot logically prove anything that is truly meaningful. Therefore, we cannot expect an explanation of the development of life to be a logical proof. We can discuss the claim that a *scientific explanation* and *a scientific proof* exist, as it were, for the development of life as a purely materialist process, devoid of God. In the next section we will see that Darwin's claim that the natural selection mechanism explains the process of the development of life on Earth has the status of a metaphysical belief. It does not have the status of a scientific theory, as many people believe, including those who consider themselves to be highly educated, rather it is a belief that is not based on any experience or logic.

4. Darwinism – a Metaphysical, not a Scientific, Hypothesis

A "scientific explanation of evolution" means that a *scientific theory* of the evolution of life on Earth exists. The main thesis of the analysis proposed below is that it is impossible to derive a scientific theory of evolution from the paleontological data that describe evolution, *on the assumption that the development of the animal kingdom is evolutionary in nature.*

Darwinism proposes a certain hypothesis, which supposedly explains the development of life on Earth. We already know (see Chapter Three, section 2) that scientific theories are hypotheses, but not all hypotheses are scientific theories. Therefore we need to check whether the Darwinist hypothesis meets the criteria of a scientific theory.

First, we will take another look at the nature of the process of the development of life according to the theory of evolution – the Darwinist hypothesis. In our analysis we will use the results of the current scientific study of the genetic mechanism that is uniform for every living creature.

Let us look first at the development of life. The first creature, the simplest and tiniest one, started to reproduce, with the mechanism that transfers all its characteristics to its offspring. Its offspring are, in fact, exact replicas of the organism. Of course, this is only on condition that the transfer of characteristics takes place without any distortions, and there are no changes in the genetic material. If this condition were actually fulfilled, then today, three-and-a-half billion years after the formation of life, only one creature would exist on Earth, with a large number of replicas. In other words, without mutations, evolution would not occur at all. And if evolution occurred up to a certain stage, and at a certain moment the mutations ceased, then from that moment evolution would have ceased, according to the evolutionary scenario accepted today.

We have come to an important conclusion, that when the genetic mechanism operates precisely, without any disturbances, then evolution is impossible. Only if there are mutations, random changes, can evolution occur. This means that according to the Darwinist hypothesis, the process of evolution is controlled by random events.

In the first section, we posed the question of whether science is capable of describing the development of the world, when it is like a historical process. There is only one world and its development is a chain of inter-connected events. We came to the conclusion that only in the event that all the events in the chain are connected by an unequivocal, deterministic causal connection is it possible to attempt to build a scientific theory for development of this kind. This was the theory of the development of the inanimate world after the Big Bang. However, as we have just seen, in the development of life on Earth – the evolution of life – randomness plays a decisive role. Darwin's theory of evolution, in its modern form, claims that randomness combined with the heredity that passes on all the random changes to the offspring of every biological entity explains all the amazing creatures of the animal kingdom, including the greatest creature of all, man.

Soon we will see that there cannot be a *scientific theory* that describes and explains all of these creations. In order to explain the appearance of these creations we must break away from the exclusively scientific approach, which we will discuss in later sections. Here I plan to expand on the naturalist, secular approach, which denies anything that is outside of the sphere of science.

Let us ponder more deeply why there can be a scientific explanation and description in the case of deterministic development, but it is impossible to provide a scientific description when it is randomness that determines the development. We can present the development of the system of life on Earth as a chain of events, starting from the appearance of the first living thing. If all the events subsequent to this were connected by a chain of causes and effects, with each cause having a singular effect, then it would be possible to talk about the law of evolution. If there is a law that connects causes and effects within the evolutionary process, then there may also be a scientific description of evolution using a theory, which is a reflection, an image of that law. According to Popper's theory of cognition (Chapter Three, section 2) it is possible to propose a hypothesis – a scientific theory – about the law that connects causes and effects, a hypothesis that can be tested by experiment. But it is not the law that determines the connection of the chain of the events of the development of life on Earth, but the *absence of the law*, chance, that connects the events of development. This is the case according to the secular, godless approach.

If we were to record the evolutionary process on film, then every replay would create a new film, showing a completely different history. With this vivid metaphor, Gould presents the idea that evolution is unpredictable. The key concept here is contingency, the dependence on prior random events:

A historical explanation does not rest on direct deduction from laws of nature, but on an unpredictable sequence of antecedent states, where any major change in any sequence would have altered the final result. This final result is therefore dependent, or contingent, upon everything that came before - the unerasable and determining signature of history.[3]

We have come to the unequivocal conclusion that *a scientific theory of evolution does not exist because a law of evolution does not exist.* From a physical perspective, the *biosphere* – the system of life on Earth – is not a closed, isolated physical system, but is affected by cosmic particles. And this is not a small insignificant effect like in the majority of the physical systems that we are familiar with. We have seen that random factors and cosmic particles have a crucial influence – without them there is no change in the biosphere. This fact is well-known to biologists who take the biosphere as a whole into account. We cited the biologist Gould earlier, and I would like to add the testimony of another famous biologist. Jacques Monod, who in 1965, together with André Lwoff and François Jacob, won the Nobel Prize for his contribution to genetic biology, writes in his book, Chance and Necessity:

The thesis I shall present in this book is that the biosphere does not contain a predictable class of objects or of events but constitutes a particular occurrence, compatible indeed with first principles, but not deducible from those principles and therefore essentially unpredictable.[4]

In addition, he writes:

I believe that we can assert today that a universal theory, however completely successful in other domains, could never encompass the biosphere, its structure, and its evolution as phenomena deducible from first principles.[5]

It is possible that the natural selection mechanism plays

---

3. *Wonderful Life*, p. 283
4. *Chance And Necessity*, p. 43
5. Ibid., p. 42

an important role in the process of the evolution of life on Earth. But there is a large jump from here to the claim that the mechanism of adaptation by natural selection *explains* the evolution of life on Earth. The general consensus is that the natural selection mechanism explains all the evolution in the world, from the moment of the formation of life (and I am purposely ignoring here the problem of the formation of life itself), and that it would apparently have been possible to predict the development of life on Earth. However, we have seen that it is impossible to make such a prediction since there is no law of evolution. *Darwinism is not a scientific theory* – all we can say is that it has the status of a metaphysical assumption. This is actually a belief that physical processes have the power of creativity – a belief that is not based on any human experience or scientific experiment.

We can conclude the analysis in this section with the words of Karl Popper:

There exists no law of evolution, only the historical fact that plants and animals change, or more precisely, that they have changed. The idea of a law which determines the direction and the character of evolution is *a typical nineteenth-century mistake, arising out of the general tendency to ascribe to the 'Natural Law' the functions traditionally ascribed to God.*[6]

In this section we arrived at a very important conclusion: There is no scientific theory of the development of life on Earth, and nor can there be, and the reason for this is quite simple. The development of life is a chain of events that do not have an unequivocal causal connection between them. In other words, there is no law of evolution. And if there is no law then it is also impossible to build a scientific theory of the

---

6. *Conjectures and Refutations*, p. 340; emphasis mine.

development of life and no hypotheses about the evolution of life in this world have scientific status. In the fabric of secular thought, this is an extremely significant *shortcoming*, since the secular approach considers the possibility of explaining the appearance and phenomenon of man with scientific tools to be of supreme importance.

5. Evolution and Creativity

In the previous section we came to the conclusion that the Darwinist hypothesis of the evolution of life on Earth does not have the status of a scientific theory – it has the status of a metaphysical belief. Nevertheless, one can still ask questions about the reasonableness and feasibility of this hypothesis. We shall focus on the following question: In principle, is there a possibility that a materialistic process, such as development that is based on the natural selection mechanism, is capable of leading to the creation of man?

Let us understand what we are talking about here. A very long time ago our world contained only matter; there was no life and no human beings. This material world developed according to the laws of nature, laws which do not unequivocally determine the development, in which random factors also play a part. One can say that the development of the world occurs by a combination of lawfulness and randomness.

According to the materialist approach, the world of matter is closed and there is no external factor that affects its development. Therefore, the process of development is only capable of "creating" things that are made of matter. As we saw in Chapter One, according to this approach, man is the product of material evolution, a quintessentially materialistic process that is based on a combination of lawfulness and chance. We quoted the biologist Simpson in the Epilogue to his book, *The Meaning of Evolution*:

Man is the result of a purposeless and materialistic process that did not have him in mind. He was not planned. He is state of matter, a form of life, a sort of animal, and a species of the order primates, akin nearly or remotely to all of life and indeed to all that is material.

As we mentioned above, we shall ask ourselves whether the materialistic process that is based on the natural selection mechanism is capable of leading to the creation of man. We shall start from the premise that there is no limit to the ability of the natural selection mechanism to create different things from matter. One just needs to wait a long enough period of time – and there is plenty of time, 3.5 billion years – until the "blind watchmaker" produces all the things that fill the animal kingdom. As we stated above, there is no logical or scientific proof for this, but many biologists believe in the great power of the natural selection mechanism. Even though, in my opinion, the idea that a natural, physical, materialistic process is capable of forming new creations is absurd, let us assume, for the sake of the discussion, that a materialistic process can indeed produce new creations – this is a belief in an evolution that is governed by a mechanism of natural selection.

But before we continue with the discussion on "the creativity of nature" we shall take a moment to consider the concept of creativity in general. What is a creation? We all know intuitively what a creation is. A creation is something special, unique. A true creation is a completely new thing which does not come from something that already exists. But the creation's being original is only a necessary condition – it is not sufficient. The statement $871 + 3675 = -31$ is unique and does not derive from any arithmetical statement, but it is not a creation. Specialness is, without a doubt, an important quality, but there needs to be something else – a creation must also be appropriate to something. This statement is not appropriate to anything, hence it is not creative. In contrast, the statement $3 + 5 = 8$ is appropriate to the rules of arithmetic, but it is not original and therefore it, too, is not creative.

A true creation must meet the conditions of *originality* and *appro-*

priateness. Beethoven's Fifth Symphony is both original and appropriate to the tastes of human beings. A new scientific theory, such as Einstein's theory of relativity, is *original* – it does not derive from any previous theory – and it is also *appropriate* to experience. To use concepts from the field of probability, there is no probability of achieving a true creation randomly, simply by guessing. We saw in Chapter Three, section 2, that the chance of discovering a new scientific theory is practically zero. This can be illustrated if we imagine a large wall on which a point in a tiny circle is drawn. The probability that an arrow that is shot from afar will land precisely on that point is negligible, but when we shoot arrows randomly at the wall, we will obviously hit some point on it, even though the probability of reaching that particular point is also negligible. In this example, any point on the wall is analogous to a thing that is original but is not appropriate to a particular condition or criterion. Every time that we shoot an arrow it strikes something that is rare but not creative. Conversely, it is impossible – the probability is minute, and as matter of fact zero, if there is a continuum of points – to hit the point marked in the circle by a random shot of the arrow. This is analogous to a creation (it is original, since the probability of achieving it randomly is negligible, and it is appropriate, which is symbolized by the circle).

Now, we will ignore the negligible probability of true creations, and we shall assume, for the sake of the discussion, that the evolution of life that is operated by the natural selection mechanism does create many creations. Which resources can this process use? Which materials are at its disposal? All its resources, according to the secular-materialist view, are material – matter that functions according to the laws of nature. For the sake of comparison, let us remember that human beings have created a wide variety of creations from matter, simple tools such as wheels, tables and chairs, as well as complex machines such as telephones, record players, radios and televisions, power stations, computers, cars and many more. Man can also build all sorts of robots, which are capable of learning and improving their functioning over time. What all these inventions have in common is that they are made from matter and their functioning is determined by the laws of nature. According to the secular approach, this should also be the case with the creations of the evolutionary process. A materialistic process, with no intervention from a non-material factor, is capable, according to the Darwinist assumption, of creating a variety of different creations. These creations must be made from matter and must function solely according to the laws of nature. This is the inevitable conclusion of the assumption that the evolution of life is a natural process that occurs without the involvement of a non-material factor.

The crucial difference between man and an entity that operates solely according to the laws of nature becomes apparent when we look at man's *free will* and his quality of creativity. Here the poverty of secularism, in its attempt to describe the phenomenon of man, becomes blatantly clear.

But this discovery of the poverty of secularism comes at a price – we have to assume the existence of free will. We pointed out in Chapter Two, section 5, that this is a metaphysical assumption which cannot be proven or refuted by logic or experiment. I am completely convinced that I have free will, but anyone who flies the banner of naturalism (and holds that view consistently) could claim that there is no free will and that all of man's actions are exclusively determined by the laws of nature. One must understand that man's most remarkable quality, that which distinguishes him from all other creatures – his creativity – cannot be put into practice without free will. The inevitable conclusion of the consistent secular approach is that if man is the product of a materialist evolutionary process, then he has neither free will nor creativity, and anything that appears to be either of these qualities is actually determined by the laws of nature. The precise character of the laws of nature – whether they are deterministic like in the classical theory or non-deterministic as in quantum physics – is not important. When the laws of nature exclusively determine man's actions, then there is room for neither free will nor creativity.

In the previous section we came to the important conclusion that there is no law of evolution and therefore there cannot be a *scientific* theory of the development of life. In this section we have reached a conclusion that is no less important: Regardless of the non-existence of a scientific description of evolution, the materialistic-evolutionary process is not capable of leading to the creation of man, who is endowed with free will and creativity.

Many scientists are aware that there is a problem with a purely materialist process that leads to numerous creations and to the creation of man who is endowed with self-consciousness. Like many other phenomena (instincts, emotions etc.) consciousness is not related to matter, to *materia*. So they talk about an *emergent* evolutionary process, in which new characteristics that did not exist in the original matter are created during the development[7]. Even though the new characteristics are not derived from the physical laws that determine the evolutionary development, they suppose that the *emergent* laws are something characteristic of all the physical systems when they reach a certain level of complexity. It is easy to see that this is an attempt to overcome a genuine problem for the secular view, by the use of words, the problem of the appearance of new things, new creations in the world – *ex nihilo* – which indicates the openness of the world to God.

One cannot ignore the fact that during the evolutionary process a wide variety of new entities are created, including life itself, animals, and man with his own special characteristics and his many, unique creations of his own. The use of the

---

7. See, for example, D.M Armstrong, *A Materialist Theory of the Mind*

concept "emergent properties" is widespread amongst philosophers who discuss the evolution of life. Even Karl Popper, who does not identify with materialism and even criticizes it, talks about "creative, emergent evolution."[8] But to Popper's credit, it should be said that he does understand that inventing new words does not solve the problem. In Chapter Three, section 4, I quoted Popper saying that the greatest riddle of cosmology is that "the universe is, in a sense, creative: that it created life, and from it mind - our consciousness - which illuminates the universe, and which is creative in its turn..." It is clear that when a secular philosopher uses the word *riddle* (or *miracle*), he is confessing that the secular view cannot understand, grasp and explain the creation of new entities in the process of evolution. It is worth paying attention to the terminology and language employed by secular philosophers and scientists – the world or evolution itself produces creations. Again, we see the idolatrous outlook common to secularism – the deification of nature, claiming that it is creative. In fact, the fact that during the evolution of life new things appear *from nothing* points to the fact that the world of matter is not closed, but is open to an external authority, to a creative God (see also Chapter Three, section 4). The new things that appear during the development of the world are the creations of the creator.

6. Proofs that an Evolutionary Process in a Closed World Cannot Lead to the Creation of Man

In the previous sections we brought an argument showing the inability of a materialistic evolutionary process to lead to the creation of man on Earth. This would be sufficient if it were not for the fact that the belief in the omnipotence of the materialistic evolutionary process is so widespread. This belief

---

8.   K.R. Popper and J.C. Eccles: *The Self and Its Brain*, p. 22

is in fact at the very heart of the secular worldview. Hence I do not think it excessive to bring another argument. By the way, with regard to the concept of "proof" – we have stated several times that metaphysical claims cannot be proven or refuted. There is no doubt that this is true, but it is possible to prove that a particular metaphysical statement is not compatible with another metaphysical statement – and hence it is possible to prove that it is incorrect if we assume the correctness of the other metaphysical statement.

Man, who is endowed with free will, cannot be a product of a natural evolutionary process that proceeds according to the laws of nature. We have discussed the fact that free will is a foreign thing in a world governed solely by the laws of nature – a world that fits with the secular worldview. We have also seen the limitations and weakness of this view, which actually denies the most important human ability, that of creativity. A consistent secular analysis leads to this conclusion, even if not everyone is aware of this. Therefore, if we assume that man is indeed endowed with free will, then it follows that a natural evolutionary process is not capable of leading to his creation.

A person who functions as a sophisticated computer cannot be the paradigm for a real person.

What does this mean? According to the secular view man is part of nature, and he therefore functions solely according to the laws of nature. In principle, one can liken man's brain to a highly sophisticated computer. Man, and in particular his brain, operates and functions in accordance with the laws of physics. Even when it is occupied, say, with a mathematical theory, it still operates according to the laws of physics. Amongst other things, as a mathematician, man (who, according to the secular view is no more than an elaborate computer) can infer mathematical statements from the premises of the system – from its axioms. Now we can compare the man-computer with real

Gödel's theorem

When one considers mathematical theories one can get the impression that it is possible to establish mathematics on a firm base, and that mathematical truths can be inferred through logical actions, algorithms. An algorithm is a finite series of well-defined logical actions. In the context of the computer, an algorithm is a logical and finite series of instructions (commands) that are contained in a particular piece of software. David Hilbert, one of the most important mathematicians of the start of the twentieth century, believed that all mathematical truths could be inferred through algorithms. He did not prove his hypothesis, and actually left it as one of the unsolved problems. If this hypothesis is correct, and a procedure really exists that enables us to solve mathematical problems using algorithms, then a computer, if it is sophisticated enough, and the human brain, which is the most sophisticated computer in the world, would be capable of solving all mathematical problems.

Hilbert's program, an algorithmic structure of all of mathematics, failed when a brilliant Austrian mathematician, Kurt Gödel, proved his remarkable theorem, Gödel's theorem. He answered Hilbert's question of whether, in principle, a procedure exists by which all the mathematical problems could be solved one after the after, and the answer was, no!

Gödel proved that in every mathematical system of axioms and rules of proof of theorems, there are statements that it is impossible to prove or refute. The only assumption is that the system is rich enough and contains arithmetical rules or theorems. Gödel proved that there are mathematical truths that cannot be arrived at using algorithmic operations.

man[9]. In order to make the comparison between real man and his secular model – the elaborate computer, we shall use one of the most important mathematical discoveries: Gödel's theorem.

The comparison between the model of man based on the secular concept that man is simply an elaborate computer, and actual man, leads to an unequivocal conclusion: Actual man can "see" truths that the computer-man cannot "see". Other than statements that can be logically inferred (using algorithms), there are truths that actual man is capable of "seeing" while computer-man, because of his limitations, cannot attain them. This is what Gödel proved. In other words, scientific tools are not enough to describe, understand and explain the phenomenon called man. Of course, actual man's qualities are numerous and diverse – they are not limited to seeing mathematical truths. Man is capable of discovering wonderful creations which no computer would be able to produce, but Gödel's theorem does enable us to *prove logically* that man has the ability to discern mathematical truths which a computer is unable to deduce. Again, we come to the conclusion that there is a "gap" in the secular view of man, which cannot be overcome without stepping *outside* of its domain.

Now I intend to significantly relax the demands of the evolutionary process that leads to the formation of man. In the previous section we spoke about an *emergent* or *creative* evolutionary process. In fact, this is the true evolutionary process that is accompanied by numerous creations, including the creation of man, but it is described using a concept that, apparently explains the creativity of the process. We said earlier that inventing words cannot solve the real problem of explaining a process which, inherently, is not compatible with the secular view, and even contradicts it. However, let us

---

9. For a comprehensive discussion of this topic see J.R. Lucas, *The Freedom of the Will.*

ignore for a moment the lack of consistency in this view, and let us assume, for the sake of argument, that man was in fact created as a result of an emergent evolutionary process, and we will prove the following statement.

In a closed world, man is not able to be a scientist who discovers the laws of nature. Earlier, in Chapter Three, which dealt with knowledge of the world, we discussed the incorrectness of the principle of induction: It is impossible to infer a new scientific theory and to discover new laws of nature based on empirical data, observations and logical analysis alone. This was the philosophical finding of the Scottish philosopher David Hume. His discovery created a problem: How can we reconcile the existence of science with the inability to infer the laws of nature from observation of nature? In Chapter Three we saw that this is a mystery that has no solution within the secular view, which assumes – explicitly or implicitly – that the world is closed, meaning that nature and man (who himself is a part of nature) are all that there is. And if it is impossible to infer the laws of science from data from experiments in nature, then the very existence of science is a miracle for the secular thinker. We have seen that the solution lies in the openness of the world to God, but for the secular thinker, the world is closed. In such a world, man is not capable of discovering the laws of nature – and this is what we mean by the statement that we have proven here.

Of course, in a closed world man is also incapable of being a prophet or an artist – he is not able to create anything that is truly new. However, I decided to write the sentence at the start of the previous paragraph as I did specifically in order to highlight the scientist, and the reason for this is simple. In an argument with a secular thinker we have to take into account his opposing argument. He may deny that a work of art is something that is unique and that does not derive from anything that preceded it, and he will of course deny the phenomenon of prophecy and the existence of prophets. But he cannot deny the existence of new scientific theories. It is actually possible to prove that the theory of relativity or quantum theory are not derived from any scientific theories that came before them. One can prove that scientific theories are indeed true creations. However, even though I firmly believe that Beethoven's Fifth Symphony is a true creation, I cannot prove it.

In this section we have presented three statements that are not compatible with the secular view, that contradict it and reveal a substantial hole in the very heart of the fabric of secular thought.

7. The Evolution of Life – a Providential Process

Let us conclude. The naturalist view leads to the clear conclusion of the randomness of the process of the development of life, and hence there is no possibility of describing this process scientifically[10]. Science is not capable of describing and explaining the creative process that has led to such a large amount of diverse creations. If we want to understand the development of life on Earth we must move away from the secular, naturalist approach, that is devoid of God.

Prior to Darwin's discoveries, it was commonly thought, or should I say believed, that the animal kingdom, with all of its diversity, is the fruit of God's design. The British theologian, William Paley, in his book *Natural Theology* (1802), used scientific data to present the argument from design. If we found a watch, even on a desert island, the harmony

---

10. Of course, science is also capable of describing random processes statistically, when there is a collection of identical systems. But we have only one planet Earth.

between the parts of the watch would force us, so Paley claims, to deduce that it was made by a skilled watchmaker. Paley goes on to ask whether since the human eye is so much more complex than a watch, it is possible that it does not have a creator. This argument made a strong impression. It was clear to all that complex and sophisticated design was required for the creation of animals and plants. And here Darwin has proposed a "scientific", materialist explanation for the development of life on Earth. The creation of the plants and animals, including human beings, was carried out by nature, as it developed. However, we saw above that this claim is not true – a natural process without an additional force is not capable of creating a creature that has free will and creativity. It is worth noting that from the point of view of a consistent secular philosopher, the phenomenon of creation is the greatest mystery in the world. In Chapter Three, section 4, we saw Karl Popper's comments:

I would even suggest that the greatest riddle of cosmology may well be neither the original big bang, nor the problem why there is something rather than nothing... but that the universe is, in a sense, creative: that it created life, and from it mind - our consciousness - which illuminates the universe, and which is creative in its turn...Einstein said something like this: "If there were not this internal illumination, the universe would merely be a rubbish heap."

We have come to the unequivocal conclusion that *Darwinism does not have the status of a scientific theory*, but that of a pagan, idolatrous belief in the creativity of nature. This is a belief that nature not only creates many diverse creations, but it does this in a progressive order – first the simple creations and then the more complex ones, up until the most complex and sophisticated of all, human beings. It is as though the concept of progress is inherent within nature. Darwin himself, ultimately came to the conclusion that it is impossible to explain evolutionary progress within the framework of the theory of evolution. On December 4, 1872, he wrote to his friend

Alpheus Hyatt: "After long reflection, I cannot avoid the conviction that no innate tendency to progressive development exists."[11]

To a serious philosopher (such as Karl Popper) who ignores the existence of God, the creativity of nature is an enigma and a mystery. The belief that a creation can be created without a creator is an unfounded belief, which does not rely on any facts. On the contrary, our accumulated experience clearly shows that no creation exists without a creator. It is true that modern physics provides us with examples of phenomena that contradict our day-to-day experience. However, other things being equal, while there are no facts that contradict our common sense, we should rely on it.

The concept of evolution applies to every slow, gradual change in personality or reality, physical or spiritual. One can think of two *paradigms* of development. Let us start with the first type of development. This development takes place according to the laws of nature, where the developing system is an active party in its own development. The cosmological theory of the Big Bang describes this kind of development. The laws of physics in general and Einstein's equations of the general theory of relativity in particular describe the development of the universe. At the moment of creation, the universe was entirely concentrated in one minuscule point, and then an explosion took place, the universe spread out, and galaxies, stars and planets were formed, among them, planet Earth. The laws of physics seemingly describe this process. I say "seemingly" since this description is actually nothing but a research program and is not a real physical description. Physics does not know how to describe a universe that is concentrated in one point. The laws of physics with which we are familiar are not capable of describing matter or energy concentrated in an extremely small space. Nonetheless, we are able to imagine that a particular stage in the development of the world is controlled by the laws of

---

11. Quoted from *Wonderful Life* by S.J. Gould; p. 257

physics. This stage includes neither the "first moment" (the creation of the world, as we clarified in Chapter One, does not belong to the realm of science at all) nor the present reality, in which man's choices influence development, in addition to the laws of physics.

The stage of the evolution of life, too, cannot only be described as a derivative of the laws of nature. To aptly describe this stage in the development of the world, we can use human life as a paradigm. Over the course of his life man makes numerous decisions and choices according to his own will, while the laws of physics, chemistry and biology work alongside them. But they do not exclusively determine the development of man's life. It is man's soul that determines the important events in his life. What is different about this paradigm is the change due to the action of a factor external to the material system, which presides over the development as a whole. This factor is man's soul. A description using the paradigm of human life is only an analogy that can be understood in human terms. In the analogy man's soul represents God who supervises the development of the world. When we consider reality as a whole and its creative development, we come to the conclusion that there are not, in fact, two paradigms. There is one singular process of development of the world, and it takes place under divine providence. The closest analogy for us, human beings, is the life of man. The paradigm of development that is controlled solely by the laws of nature may be useful as an approximation to the development of the world at a certain stage and within a limited time-period. However, even as an approximation, this paradigm is not suitable to the stage of evolution of life, since the evolution of life cannot be described as happening solely via the laws of nature. Furthermore, we saw earlier that according to the modern scientific viewpoint, the development of life is not determined solely by the laws of nature, but is in the realm of randomness, the realm of the absence of physical lawfulness. From our point of view, it is not chance but divine providence that determines the development of life.

In Chapter Three, section 4 we mentioned the close connection between the phenomenon of creation and divine providence. A true creation is always something new that does not derive from something that already exists. This is something that does not come from our world but from outside of it, which is expressed in the concept "*ex nihilo*" – *nihilo* refers to the fact that it does not belong to our world. A true creation requires the openness of the world to divine providence and God's intervention. The creation of law and order in the world also belongs to divine creation, as it is the setting of the stage, the framework for divine activity. Hence, if we are looking for signs of divine activity in the development of the world, we must pay attention to the creations that appear during the process. We must rid ourselves of the pagan view, which deifies nature and attributes the quality of creativity to it. The development of life is accompanied by a remarkable creation of an abundance of living creatures and plants. From the analysis in this chapter it is clear that it is not chance that causes this incredible creation, but it is He who created the heavens and the Earth – the Creator.

CHAPTER FIVE: THE HISTORY OF MAN

1. The Era of Man

Up to this point we have been trying to understand the world in which we live. This issue is important for the formation of our worldview, however, the most important thing for man to understand is the meaning of his life. To understand the meaning of life it is also important to understand the processes of the creation and development of the world, but most important is that man understand his position vis-ú-vis the Creator. A new era began with the creation of man, and understanding the importance of this era may bring us closer to understanding the meaning of each of our individual lives. In this chapter we shall focus on human history, both from a Jewish-religious perspective and from a secular perspective. We shall focus on the most important subject for all human beings: the meaning of life. We shall study this subject, too, through a Jewish-religious lens and from the secular point of view.

What characterized the development of the world during the long period prior to the creation of man? It must be the case that it was exclusively contingent on the will of the Creator. Needless to say, divine providence exists simultaneously with the operation of the laws of nature, since the laws of nature and their operation are also part of providence. In Chapter Two, section 5, we noted that the entire creation without man functioned in complete harmony with the will of the Creator. The creation of man was a kind of revolution. A creature was created that was not obliged to act according to the will of the Creator, *but was free to act according to its own will*. Man has free will.[1]

With man's appearance in the global arena, a new era began – the era of human history. It is worth noting that when we talk about the start of a new era we mean that a new thing appeared at a particular place in the world, while the rest of the world (apart from that place) remains in the old era. So we say that a new era began when life was formed on Earth, even though there were no signs of life outside of Earth. The importance of the new era is not measured by the size of the space in which it exists, but in the originality, complexity and sophistication of the new thing that has begun to exist, wherever it may be.

The uniqueness of the era of history lies in the fact that man's will started to be an important factor in the development of the world. Prior to the creation of man the world was governed by providence and by the laws of nature, which are themselves a part of providence. From a secular perspective, which denies the existence of providence, the development of the world was determined solely by the laws of nature. As we mentioned in the previous section, the hypothesis that the world develops solely according to the laws of nature can be reasonable as an approximation for the development of the world in the period after the Big Bang, but prior to the formation of life. In the era before the creation of man, from a secular perspective, the evolution of life was contingent on the existence of random processes, without which there would not have been any development. Hence, the great creativity of the period of evolution is attributable to the combination of law and chance, which is in fact the

---

1. Of course, other creatures also have the ability to choose between various options in order to satisfy their needs. However, a human being has a conscious freedom of will at a higher level – not only can he fulfill his responsibilities and overcome his instincts, he can also make those rare choices that bring about the creation of new things.

absence of law. As we have seen, this is not a scientific view, but a metaphysical belief which is not based on any fact and which contradicts the existence of man's free will.

A study of the era of man amplifies the difficulty in understanding the historical processes that are governed solely by natural factors, as is claimed by the secular view. From our perspective, there is a spiritual cause – man's will – that affects the historical development. Perhaps not everyone appreciates the fact that the price of consistently adhering to the secular view is the complete denial of free will. The implication of this denial is the attribution of outstanding human creativity solely to natural forces – to the laws of nature and to chance.

However, we have absolutely no reason to restrict ourselves to the ridiculous belief in the omnipotence of the laws of nature and chance, and in their creative powers. Therefore we shall focus for now on understanding the processes that are governed by providence and man's will, as an alternative to the secular-naturalist view. In the following two sections we shall concentrate on understanding the historical development that is managed by divine providence and is open to the wills of human beings. Only afterwards will we return to the discussion of the limitations of secular thought.

2. Non-determinism of the World Open to God and the Will of Man

Deterministic processes, in which everything is pre-determined, are relatively easy to understand. One can compare the world that is governed solely by the laws of nature to a perfectly accurate watch, the positions of the hands of which can be predicted for every future moment and for all time. However, we saw in Chapter Two, section 4, that the true (quantum) laws of nature do not unequivocally determine the future of the world, which highlights the lack of determinism in the development of the world. In Chapter Two, section 4, we also noted that there is no meaningful difference between classical determinism and quantum non-determinism: in both cases everything is determined by material components of the world, by *materia* and the movements of the particles that comprise all things. The existence or non-existence of prior knowledge of the development of matter is only a secondary issue. In the classical scenario, in principle, it is possible to know in advance and to predict the future at every stage of development, while in the quantum scenario it is not possible to precisely predict the future. However, in both scenarios the movement of *materia determines* everything, and providence and man's choice play no role. Hence, the word determinism can apply equally to all development that is exclusively determined by the laws of nature.

True non-determinism is linked to the influence and intervention of providence in the processes of the development of the world in general, and to providence and man's will in the processes of history in particular. This is much more difficult to comprehend than the (imaginary) development that is determined purely by the laws of nature. The difficulty lies in understanding the effect of a spiritual cause on the movements of matter, a topic that we dealt with in Chapter Two, section 6. Now, let us think about the concept of the *future* in a world that is open to divine providence and the wills of man. Is it possible to predict the future in such a non-deterministic world? Is it even possible to talk about the future in such a world? Is it possible to define the future as something that belongs to the world? The answer is that the future of the world is not determined by its past, but rather God and man determine each step of its development. The future is not pre-determined; it is also contingent on the acts of each and every one of us, at every moment – it is also dependent on us.

Only by assuming that all of development is determined by deterministic laws is it possible to talk about a defined future. However, we can only use this assumption as an approximation and only in simple, abstract circumstances, such as the movements of the celestial bodies in the solar system. Generally speaking, the concept of the future is not defined, and does not derive causally and unequivocally from everything that took place in the past and in the present. The development of the world is a sequence of new events which were not determined at the beginning of days. "And the Lord saw that the wickedness of man was great in the earth, and that every imagination of the thoughts of his heart was only evil continually. And it repented the Lord that He had made man on the earth, and it grieved Him at His heart." (Genesis 6:5-6) "And the earth was corrupt before God, and the earth was filled with violence." (Genesis 6:11) These verses clearly show that the reality that was created was not latent in the act of creation but was the result of the deeds of man, the result of his free will.

"If you walk in my statutes, and keep my commandments, and do them, then I will give your rains in their season, and the land shall yield her produce, and the trees of the field shall yield their fruit... But if you will not hearken unto me, and will not do all these commandments... I also will do this unto you: I will appoint terror over you... And your strength shall be spent in vain; for your land shall not yield her produce, neither shall the trees of the land yield their fruit." (Leviticus 26:3-20) The Torah states very clearly, both here and in many other places, that the reality that will take place *in the future* is contingent on the deeds of man, and these deeds are the outcomes of his choices.

If this is the case then we can conclude that the word *future* does not express any entity that exists in our world. There is only a changing reality. In principle, nothing is definite about what is going to happen in the next moment – neither on a personal level nor on a global level. On a personal level, we know that every moment in our lives could be our last. Both the existence of the world and the existence of time itself are constantly dependent on God's will. All that we can say is that the world, and human beings within it, are constantly changing and developing and the result of this development is the future. But there is absolutely no certainty about what will happen in the world even at the very next moment – this is dependent on God's will, on man's choices, on this moment and on the moments preceding it. Therefore, any attempt to present the future as something that is defined and exists, as something that can be predicted or foreseen, is doomed to failure. However, this does not contradict the fact of God's design, or God's plan. We will discuss this in the next section.

3. Human History – Divine Planning and Free Will

Human beings carry out historical processes, but it is God who plans and directs them. Divine providence is one of the most important principles of Judaism. God is involved in man's affairs and manages history – He is the God of history. The first of the Ten Commandments is: "I am the Lord your God, who brought you out of the land of Egypt, out of the house of bondage." (Exodus 20:2) Another important principle is that human beings have free will. The history of humankind is a story of God's coping with human beings who have free will and are His partners in the creation of history. The Jewish approach to history is summarized by Rabbi Akiva: "Everything is foreseen, but the freedom of choice is given." (Ethics of the Fathers 3:15) This saying expresses the essence of human history.

Philosophers have tried to overcome the problem that lies, in their opinion, in the contradiction between the two parts of this statement: on the one hand everything is foreseen, while at the same time the freedom of choice is given[2]. The first part seems to describe absolute determinism,

2. In my book *Creation Ex Nihilo*, I presented a summary of the opinions of Jewish

while the second part expresses the non-determinism that is related to man's free will. "Everything is foreseen" apparently expresses the power, the omnipotence and the omniscience of divine providence. If God knows everything that is going to happen – if everything is foreseen – where does man's free will fit in?

I believe that at least some of the above claims derive from foreign sources, and not from the Torah. The idea that God's omnipotence also includes omniscience does not come from the Torah at all. Furthermore, the Torah stresses, in numerous places, that its prophecy is always *conditional* on man's actions. In the previous section we saw that all reality is contingent, conditional, dependent on God's will and man's actions. From here it becomes clear that the concept of the *future* is not defined as an entity that already exists at the present time, an entity that can be either known or not known. In contrast to the *past*, which has already been fixed by the development that occurred prior to the present, the *future* is open to both man's and God's involvement. Put simply, I would say that it is impossible to know something that does not exist.

If this is the case, how can we understand the phrase "everything is foreseen"? In my opinion, this is talking about *the divine plan*. "Everything is foreseen" means that sooner or later, in one way or another, "the counsel of the Lord will stand", with the method and time of implementation being dependent on man's actions and choices. "Everything is foreseen" does not cancel out man's free will, the opposite is the case: man is an active partner with God in the *creation* of the future. Whether the redemption comes "at the appointed time or sooner" depends on us, human beings. It is man who carries out historical processes, but under God's supervision. The real secret, which human beings are unable to comprehend, is how God implements His plan despite people's different wills and desires.

Rabbi Akiva's paradox "Everything is foreseen yet the freedom of

philosophers on this topic.

choice is given" is not about God's knowledge of every detail of the future versus the individual's free will. As we have already stated, it is impossible to know something that does not exist. *The secret lies in the fact that history develops in a defined direction and towards a goal set in advance by God, even though human beings have differing and sometimes even contradictory wills. The secret is how God manages to direct and manage historical processes.*

To summarize: The future of the world and of humanity was not defined and determined at the beginning of days. The future of the world is constantly *dependent* on God's will and man's actions. Freedom of choice is given to man in his role as God's partner in the creation of humanity's future, while the fulfillment of God's counsel, of the divine plan, is assured: everything is foreseen.

4. The Secular Approach to History

Human history has meaning. Divine providence determines the direction of the development of humanity and its goal. In Judaism, God is the God of history and His commandments have historical meaning. Man is God's partner in the shaping of humanity, and there is a reciprocal relationship between God and man in the process of development. On the other hand, history without any divine guidance, as in the secular view, is also without value or meaning. But one should not think that a secular philosopher would agree with this conclusion regarding the absurdity of godless historical processes. On the contrary, many secular thinkers try to attribute inherent meaning to history. But soon we shall see that a consistent analysis of the secular approach leads unequivocally to the conclusion that godless history is meaningless.

The secular view of history is not uniform and one can see two opposing trends within it. According to one fairly widely held view, one can attribute lawfulness and directionality to history. History has its own internal meaning and internal, inherent laws which are peculiar to it, and we can attribute the concepts of progress and development to it. We learned in Chapter Two, section 3, about a similar view: the deification of nature, or the idolization of nature, but these are in fact not different views at all, since history is also a part of nature. The tendency to ascribe to history human or divine spiritual concepts is, as we have discussed, quite common. This view is very clearly expressed in the writings of Hegel, Marx, Engels and their successors, though it is not based on any logic or reason and has no scientific basis as its supporters claim.

However, there is another secular viewpoint which denies any directionality, lawfulness or meaning in historical processes. Karl Popper, in his books *The Poverty of Historicism* and *The Open Society and Its Enemies*, quite convincingly criticizes the first approach, the one that idolizes history. Without doubt, within the context of a secular approach, this critique is consistent and well-founded. Jacques Monod, too, in his book *Chance and Necessity*, comes to the conclusion that one cannot find meaning in human history. A godless worldview will consistently lead to conclusions of the meaninglessness of human history and the absurdity of life.

We have two opposing secular worldviews, so let us look at them one by one. Marxism expresses the most developed secular notion of lawfulness in history. In 1859 Marx wrote: "The mode of production in material life determines the general character of the social, political, and intellectual processes of life. It is not the consciousness of men which determines their existence; it is on the contrary their social existence which determines their consciousness."[3]

This hypothesis rose to the level of the *"Law of History"* and was later called *Historical Materialism*. Historical development is determined by economic conditions, and in particular by the development of means

---

3. Preface to *Contribution to the Critique of Political Economy*

of production. We do not need to go into the ins and outs of historical materialism as it is formulated in the writings of Marx and his successors. What is important to us is the claim that there is a scientific theory that maintains that a law of history exists which determines all past historical development, as well as enabling us to predict future development.

This is where Karl Popper's critique comes into play. The very same arguments that led him (and us) to the conclusion that there is no law of evolution (see the previous chapter) are also valid for the non-existence of the law of history. Any scientific theory must be tested by facts or experiments. To form a preference for one hypothesis over another there must be a possibility of rejecting the hypothesis that is incorrect. However, with history, including the historical natural sciences, such as geological history, the facts that are at our disposal are limited and we cannot repeat them at will. A hypothesis that cannot be tested by new facts is not a scientific theory. Therefore it is impossible to establish a scientific historical theory that explains the past and can predict future development.

Popper's argument states that it is impossible to establish a scientific theory of history, but he does not say that a law of history does not exist. He claims that even if such a law does exist, we do not have the tools to discover it and to build its theory. But we can prove even more than this – we can prove that a law of history does not exist at all. Divine providence operates in many different ways, and we, human beings, cannot know God's ways. However, there is one channel that we can assume that providence uses. The development of humanity is dependent on the knowledge available to human beings. It is easy to see that if humankind were to lose its world of accessible knowledge, Popper's world three, then it would return to the position it was in thousands of years ago. Clearly it is not only scientific knowledge, in the sense of modern science, that affects historical developments; knowledge in general also has an impact on history. Before modern science developed, the human race came up with numerous innovations that dramatically influenced its development. One only needs to mention examples such as the invention of the wheel, the development of agriculture and the like. But we should not think that it is only scientific and technological ideas that affect humanity. The influence of religious, social and artistic ideas is no less profound, and possibly even more so.

It is interesting to see that there is agreement among secular thinkers about the effect of knowledge on the course of history. Karl Popper writes: "The truth of this premise must be admitted even by those who see in our ideas, including our scientific ideas, merely by-products of material developments of some kinds or other."[4] For example, the appearance or invention of a new production tool *first takes place on the spiritual level*, and only at a later stage is the idea realized into a material object.

Up to this point we have given a factual account of the effect of knowledge on historical development. Secular philosophers and religious individuals have drawn wildly differing conclusions from this account. From the fact that the abundance of knowledge affects the course of history, Karl Popper draws the conclusion that there is no lawfulness, directionality or meaning in human history. He argues his point in the Foreword to his book, *The Poverty of Historicism*, thus:

The course of human history is strongly influenced by the growth of human knowledge.

We cannot predict, by rational or scientific methods, the future growth of our scientific knowledge. (This assertion can be logically proved).

We cannot, therefore, predict the future course of human history.

... There can be no scientific theory of historical development serving as a basis for historical prediction.

---

4. *The Poverty of Historicism*, vi

Elsewhere, (see Chapter Three, section 3) Popper states, as does Einstein, that every discovery of new knowledge is the greatest miracle in the world. A consistent secular analysis must conclude that there is no order to the discoveries of new information, and hence there is no order in the processes of history. It also follows that if there is no internal order and no lawfulness in history, then human history also has no meaning. We must recognize the fact that the absurdity of life and the meaninglessness of history are conclusions that follow from a consistent secular approach, which ignores divine providence.

So what is our conclusion? What is the religious view? In Chapter Three, we saw that every discovery of new knowledge is in fact a divine revelation. That is to say, new knowledge enters the consciousness of humankind from God and according to His plan. The meaning of life and the meaning of history are determined by God, in accordance with His will. We, human beings, are not capable of comprehending the divine plan and all its details. Our knowledge only comes from the revelations that God provides to us.

We can conclude that a consistent analysis leads to an unequivocal conclusion: There is no internal, inherent law of history. History is not an entity that has internal laws. Both secular and religious thinkers accept this statement, but their conclusions differ enormously. It is clear that according to the view that ignores the existence of God, history has no meaning if it has no internal lawfulness. In contrast, according to the religious approach there is only one source of meaning in history, and that source is God.

CHAPTER SIX: THE MEANING OF LIFE

1. "Under the Sun" – The Secular Analysis of the Meaning of Life

In this section we shall continue to discuss the secular view that denies the existence of a God who governs the world and man within it. According to the secular view, the entire world is nature, and everything in it, including human beings, is a product of nature and its development. There is nothing above nature. Therefore, it is clear that nature alone (without God and man) has no meaning or value. About this there is no disagreement between the Torah and the secular thinker. The Torah emphasizes that man is the center of the world: "No shrub of the field was yet in the earth, and no herb of the field had yet sprung up; for the Lord God had not caused it to rain upon the earth, and there was not a man to till the ground." (Genesis 2:5). Rashi explains that the purpose of creation was that man would be created to pray for the rains that would fall and water the trees and shrubs. And Rabbi Soloveitchik concludes: "Nature on its own, without man, is somewhat absurd. The world needs man who prays, and only with his appearance does growth begin." (*Man and His World*, p.280 (in Hebrew))

Also, from the secular perspective a world without man has no meaning – the existence of such a world is absurd. In Chapter Three, section 4, we quoted Albert Einstein: "If there were not this internal illumination [of man], the universe would merely be a rubbish heap". However, according to the secular viewpoint, if we study its ramifications consistently, the world has no meaning even with man in it. According to this view man is a product of nature, and is therefore an integral part of it. And if there is no value or meaning in nature, then no meaning could have been created due to man's association with nature.

Perhaps this claim is not as self-evident as the thesis of the absurdity of a world without man (and God). So, let us look at a world in which it is man who gives meaning to his life and to the world as a whole. In a world without God, man is the sole creature to which value and meaning can be ascribed. In such a world one cannot turn to a transcendental God, who is external to the world, for values and standards. Only man can create meaning in our world. But here there is a trap. In a world in which all the values are based on human choice, anything could become a value, and this is problematic. Eliezer Berkovitz, in his article "Faith after the Holocaust", brings a quotation from Himmler's speech on the final solution. He said to the SS leaders who were gathered together: "To have gone through that, and to have remained an honest man just the same, save for the exceptions due to human nature, that is what has made you tough and strong. This is a glorious page in our history, never before, never again to be written..."[1] The Communists in Soviet Russia also brought to the world their values and ethics and caused the murders of tens of millions of innocent civilian men, women and children.

If the existence of a world without God is absurd, then the proposition that man is the sole source of meaning is also cast into doubt. In an absurd universe man is also absurd, as are the values and meaning that he invents for himself. King Solomon, the wisest of all men, dealt with the problem of the meaning of life in a world that is subject solely to the forces

---

1. *Essential Essays on Judaism*, p. 319

of nature. He expresses the absurdity of the world "under the sun", a world that lacks a divine dimension: "Vanity of vanities, says Kohelet; vanity of vanities, all is vanity. What profit has man of all his labor wherein he labors under the sun?" (Ecclesiastes 1:2-3) "Under the sun" means under the forces of nature, subject to them. There is no benefit, no purpose or goal in subjugation to the forces of nature. Under the sun there is no purpose, but above the sun there is. Kohelet examines all aspects of life without a divine dimension, with man being just a part of nature and nothing more, and he comes to the following conclusion: "For that which befalls the sons of men befalls beasts; even one thing befalls them both. As the one dies, so dies the other. Yes, they have all one breath, so that man has no pre-eminence over a beast; for all is vanity" (Ecclesiastes 3:19).

The focus of Kohelet's study is the life of a man who wants to achieve good things in this world "under the sun". This man does not particularly involve himself in his spiritual essence, in his place in the world, in the meaning of his existence and the like; these questions relate to "above the sun". Nothing that is "under the sun", which is not related to that which is beyond man's biological existence, differentiates him from an animal. All the aims of life of modern man – such as a good livelihood, a nice home, a career – if they do not have a connection to a goal that is above the sun, then they do not raise man to a status that is significantly different from that of an animal. (Of course, one cannot deny the importance of attaining the material basis required for the proper functioning of man, but this is not a goal in itself that gives meaning to man's life). Both man and animal strive to achieve the maximum pleasure, but man has more tools available to him to achieve joy and pleasure, as well as more suffering and hardship.

Secular thinkers, too, who deny the "above the sun" dimension, see man as a sophisticated animal, a product of material evolution, an absolutely materialistic process based on a combination of lawfulness and chance. Hence, they come to the conclusion of the absence of meaning and randomness in the appearance of man as a result of evolution. In the Preface, we quoted the secular scientist Simpson from the Epilogue to his book The Meaning of Evolution:

Man is the result of a purposeless and materialistic process that did not have him in mind. He was not planned. He is state of matter, a form of life, a sort of animal, and a species of the order primates, akin nearly or remotely to all of life and indeed to all that is material.

Needless to say, Simpson's claim that "man was not planned" does not derive from any scientific analysis. A similar position, and perhaps a more up-to-date one, leads Jacques Monod, the biologist and Nobel Prize winner, in his book Chance and Necessity, to the following conclusion: Since the molecular processes in evolution are random, the final result (including man) is also random: "The universe was not pregnant with life nor the biosphere with man. Our number came up in the Monte Carlo game."[2] And of course, dualism – the body and soul – is apparently an illusion.[3]

These positions lead to intellectual, conceptual and ethical anarchy. In the discussion above we came to the conclusion that man cannot arrive at absolute values by himself. As an example of this we cited the Nazis and the Communists, who espoused their own ethical systems, destructive moral systems which, when put into practice, led to many deaths. However, one can imagine that educated man, who is part of western, liberal society, is capable of coming up with a different ethics, a better one, and let us ignore for a moment the question of what is "better". Thus another Nobel Prize winner, Frances Crick, proposes, in his lecture "The Social Impact of Biology" the following values:

(a) It is not right that religious instruction should be given to young children...

2. Chance and Necessity, p. 145

3. Ibid., p. 159

(b) We cannot continue to regard all human life as sacred. The idea that every person has a soul and his life must be saved at all costs should be not allowed.

(c) If a child were considered to be legally born when two days old it could be examined to see whether it was "an acceptable member of society" (otherwise it would be destroyed).

(d) It might also be desirable to define a person as legally dead when he was past the age 80 or 85... [4]

The approach that believes in the supremacy and primacy of matter and the denial of the spirit leads not only to intellectual and moral anarchy, but also to practical anarchy. In the twentieth century Nazi Germany wrought the Holocaust on the Jewish people and brought disaster to humanity as a whole. The anti-religious regime of the Soviet Union caused millions of deaths among its own people.

From a secular perspective, man – and only man – gives life meaning. We have seen the absurdity and arbitrariness of this principle: If it is impossible to determine rationally and objectively which values are preferable – liberal western values, those of the Communists or those of the Nazis – then life has no meaning, and all values are relative and arbitrary. It is worth stopping and considering this statement in greater detail. It is difficult to assume that the many people who hold the secular viewpoint (or think that they hold it) would agree that their view does not provide meaning to their lives.

To understand this topic better, we will compare it with the uniformity of the laws of nature that we discussed in Chapter Two, section 3. In other words, let us compare the system of the laws of ethics with the system of the laws of nature. We have seen that there are two approaches to understanding the

---

4. From *Challenge*, p. 452

laws of nature – the secular approach that sees nature itself as the source of the lawfulness in nature, the deification of nature which comes from Greek philosophy, and the Jewish-religious approach that sees God as the source of nature's lawfulness. In that section we found an additional "gap" in the secular view – its inability to explain the uniformity of the laws of nature everywhere in the universe, even in places that are millions, or even billions, of light years apart. We quoted Karl Popper: "The structural homogeneity of the world seems to resist any 'deeper' explanation: it remains a mystery". The uniformity of the laws of nature clearly points to their source being external to the world, to the openness of the world to God.

Now we will take a look at the system of the laws of ethics in humankind. It is worth mentioning that there is a fundamental difference between the laws of ethics and the laws of nature. The laws of nature determine the order in the world, while the laws of ethics are a command to man telling him how to behave, but they do not force him to do so, and he is free not to obey them. As with the system of the laws of nature, there are two possibilities for the laws of ethics. The source of the lawfulness is either internal or external to humanity – the laws of ethics are a divine command. If the source of the laws of ethics is internal, then human morality is relative, and there are no standards by which one can judge one ethical approach as being preferable to another. In general, we need to understand that there are two diametrically opposed views: one is the pagan, idolatrous, polytheistic view, which sees the source of order in nature and humanity as internal, and the second is the Jewish-religious view, which sees the source of the order in the world and in humanity as external to them, in God. The system itself – nature, humanity and the world – is not capable of producing meaning and order on its own. The

Torah categorically rejects the idolatrous approach, that sees man as the source of morality: "You shall not do after all that we do here this day, every man whatever is right in his own eyes" (Deuteronomy 12:8). In fact, God determines what is good and what is bad: "Observe and hear all these words which I command you, that it may go well with you, and with your children after you for ever, when you do that which is good and right in the eyes of the Lord your God." (Deuteronomy 12:28). In the book of Judges (17:6) the moral anarchy in the land is described as follows: "In those days there was no king in Israel; every man did that which was right in his own eyes". Of course the secular thinker is free to deny God's existence, but then he will be left with the absence of meaning of life, and the lack of any standards for human morality (general, objective, universal standards, that are not dependent on man).

2. The Problem of Suffering and Evil in the World – the Holocaust

> He who accepts this world as the ultimate reality will, if his mind is realistic and his heart sensitive to suffering, tend to doubt that the good is either the origin or the ultimate goal of history.
>
> (A.J Heschel, *Between God and Man*, p. 195)

Up to now we have dealt with the weaknesses, the "gaps", in the fabric of secular thought. Now let us discuss a subject which, from a secular point of view, constitutes a weakness in the Jewish-religious approach. I am talking about the problem of evil in the world – suffering and hardship in a world governed by God, a problem that became more acute after the Holocaust of the twentieth century, when the Jewish people lost six million souls. The question that is frequently asked is this: How is it possible to believe in God after what happened to the Jewish people in the Holocaust? Or, where was God when his people were being eradicated and incinerated in the German extermination camps? We cannot escape asking the question of how we can understand the existence of evil, hardship and suffering in a world that is "very good": "And God saw every thing that He had made, and, behold, it was very good." (Genesis 1:31)

The history of the Jewish people is fraught with suffering and manifestations of evil – both on an individual and on a communal level. There was the slavery in Egypt, the destruction of the First and Second Temples, the exiles and the expulsion from Spain, to name just a few. But it seems that in the twentieth century there was a jump in the level of suffering and hardship: the Holocaust. Hence the question as to how it is possible to reconcile God's justice and the unbearable suffering of man is on the agenda more than ever before. Such a question would never occur to someone who does not believe in God – neither before nor after the fact. But a believing person simply cannot ignore it. Faith sees the hand of God in everything on Earth. Therefore a believing person cannot simply go about his daily business in the face of the question of evil in the world in general, and the Holocaust in particular.

Abraham challenged God saying: "Shall not the Judge of all the earth do justly?" Abraham's faith in God could not tolerate His unjustness. This was also a problem for Job. He suffered because his faith in God's justice was cracked. Because of his faith he was not able to accept the adversary's words about God since he regarded them as an insult to God's justice.

There have been many attempts to explain and comprehend the problem of divine providence during the Holocaust. The Holocaust is our greatest national tragedy in modern times, and there are still some survivors with us today. Many thinkers have tried to understand God's behavior in the modern era. The simplest solution, and I would even say the most simplistic one, is to say that what happened to the Jews is punishment for their sins. And even today, there are many who accept this explanation. Emil Fackenheim, himself a Holocaust survivor, devoted the majority of his thinking to the subject of the Holocaust, but his conclusions can be summarized in few lines:

Thus the Holocaust is not only a unique event: it is epoch-making. The world, just as the Jewish world, can never again be the same. The event therefore resists explanation – the historical kind that seeks causes, and the theological kind that seeks meaning and purpose. *More precisely, the better the mind succeeds with the necessary task of explaining what can be explained, the more it is shattered by its ultimate failure.*[5]

It is important to emphasize that we are talking here about the problem of *understanding* or *explaining* God's providence. In Chapter Three, which talks about knowledge of the world, we saw that we, human beings, are limited in our understanding of the world. We receive both our knowledge and our understanding as divine revelation. Hence, it is not surprising that we are unable to comprehend the ways of God and his actions, other than the events that He himself reveals to us. This view is well-known and rooted in the Jewish tradition. As it is written in Ecclesiastes: "Be not rash with your mouth, and let not your heart be hasty to utter a word before God; for God is in heaven, and you upon earth; therefore let your words be few" (Ecclesiastes 5:1). It is impossible for us to comprehend these things, since we are on the earth and God is in the heavens. "For as the heavens are higher than the earth, so are My ways higher than your ways, and My thoughts than your thoughts" (Isaiah 55:9).

But the temptation is great – there are many people who think that everyone can explain and understand the historical processes that are

---

5. E.L. Fackenheim, *The Jewish Return into History*, p. 279 (emphasis mine)

governed by God, and that no prior knowledge is required for this. It is another thing entirely when we try to understand the behavior of the tiniest particles in the world – such as electrons, photons and quarks, for which one needs to know mathematics and modern physics at a very high level, knowledge that is acquired over many years of study. Those who think this way do not realize that God's ways are infinitely more sublime and complex than the behavior of a fundamental particle, which itself cannot be grasped using the concepts from our limited experience. The Psalmist writes: "How great are your deeds, Lord, exceedingly profound are your thoughts. A simple man cannot know, nor can a fool understand this." (Psalms 92:6-7). However, this does not mean that a wise and intelligent person does understand God's thoughts and the greatness of His deeds. Rather, the psalm says that a wise person "will understand this" – he will understand the greatness and profundity of his deeds, but we are not capable of understanding the deeds themselves, and a fool does not even understand how great God's deeds are.

And if we are not capable of explaining and understanding the simplest divine thing, the most basic creation, how can we hope to understand God's ways in the most complex creation, human history? When it comes to the Holocaust that took place in our time, it is almost impossible to think about it without emotion being involved. But we must realize that it is equally impossible for us to comprehend and explain an event on a far smaller scale, namely a human tragedy of just one person. We must appreciate that it is only us, human beings, who differentiate by scale, by the varying magnitude of the injustice – someone who murders one person is less guilty than someone who murders many. We cannot compare a holocaust which happened to a whole nation with the murder of a single person. Man has justice and injustice, and that is a matter of degree. But when we are talking about God, his justice is absolute. God cannot be a little bit unjust. For Him, injustice regarding one person is just as incomprehensible and baffling as injustice with regard to millions.

As Eliezer Berkovitz writes: "With God the quantity of injustice must be immaterial."[6]

Hence, in order to understand the problem of injustice in the world there is no need to go into the horrors of the Holocaust; it is sufficient to focus on a case of injustice that affects just one individual. In the summer of 1941 the German army approached the city of Kiev, where I was born and grew up. My mother and father had to decide what to do, whether to flee the city to the east, away from the Germans, or to stay there. My father was familiar with the Germans since they had been in Kiev twenty years previously and he spoke German. They were polite people and had occasionally protected the Jews from the local anti-Semites, but my parents nonetheless decided to leave Kiev. Not long ago, I visited the museum Yad Vashem in Jerusalem, where I read a manifesto published by the German authorities in Kiev when they occupied it. The manifesto called to "the *Zhids*[7] of the city of Kiev" and advised them to gather in certain places. The end of the story is well-known – the Jews of Kiev were all annihilated. I imagined what would have happened had we stayed in Kiev and I had read this forbidding manifesto, which referred to me and all the Jews as "*Zhids*". I also imagined the horror that took place afterwards. One might suggest that this is an imaginary event, since in the end I was saved. This is true, but it is not an imaginary event. The parents of Misha Ehrlich, a close friend of mine from school, decided to stay in Kiev or simply did not manage to escape from the city. When I visited Kiev after the war I found out that Misha Ehrlich had been exterminated in Babi Yar.

This case is connected to the Holocaust, but there are many tragic events, including disease and death, that take place in our lives, that have no connection to the Holocaust. Death, the loss of a person's life, is always viewed by his friends and family as an injustice and a tragedy, regardless of

---

6. *Faith after the Holocaust*, p. 130

7. *Zhid* is a derogatory term for "Jew" in Russian.

age. It is fair to say that life is not possible without suffering, hardship and injustice – these things are inescapable. A person who, in asking *Where was God during the Holocaust?* means that there can be no injustice if God is present, can also ask the same question regarding the periods prior to and subsequent to the Holocaust: Where is God at every moment, since at every moment tragic events occur?

Let us take a look at our reality, that of human beings, on two levels – the earthly, partial level that is focused on man's life over the time granted him, and the metaphysical, eschatological, level – which deals with the world as a whole, beyond our earthly, temporary lives.

When we look at the partial reality that is "under the sun" and we ignore the world as a whole, we cannot help but notice the evil and injustice that are an integral, inseparable part of it. The suffering and injustice that we endure during our lives are to a great extent a result of human activity. Thus the Holocaust, which we discussed above, is a result of the actions of the Nazis in the Second World War. In this context it is worth us clarifying man's level of responsibility for committing wrong acts. God created man and gave him free will. With this He also gave man the responsibility for doing good or evil. One might say that in a sense the Holocaust is the consequence of the free will with which man is endowed. If God were to deny man this choice and thereby eradicate evil, then man would not be able to do evil; but then he would not be man, he would be a robot, a marionette. That is not the kind of world that God wanted to create. Divine providence happens behind the scenes, but generally speaking, man cannot understand or explain how it works.

The Torah and Jewish law deal first and foremost with man's behavior in the world "under the sun". The premises of the halakhic approach to suffering and evil, halakhic ethics, is: (a) Evil does exist and it is a very negative thing; (b) Man must not accept evil without protest or become accustomed to it – he must oppose it and fight against it; (c) One must always believe that even if man loses a battle in the war against evil, at some point in the future evil will be overcome and will disappear from the world.

Rabbi Soloveitchik summarizes our position in the world under the sun, the existence of evil and the lack of justice, as follows:

There is evil, there is suffering, there are hellish torments in this world. Whoever wishes to delude himself by diverting his attention from the deep fissure in reality, by romanticizing human existence, is nought but a fool and a fantast... Therefore, Judaism determined that man, entrapped in the depths of a frozen, fate-laden existence, will seek in vain for the solution to the problem of evil within the framework of speculative thought, for he will never find it.[8]

Finite man, who lives "under the sun", cannot discover God's absolute goodness with his partial observations. By looking at the incomplete picture that is available to man in his temporary and finite life, it is impossible for him to grasp this. Only with an eschatological view that deals with the world as a whole, beyond the earthly, temporary life, can the Creator's absolute goodness and justice be discerned. At the start of this section we quoted from the Torah, where it states that the world is "very good": "And God saw every thing that He had made, and, behold, it was very good", "[h]owever, this affirmation may be made only from the infinite perspective of the Creator"[9].

Now we can return to our discussion about secularism. At the start of this section we discussed the secular claim that faith in God contradicts the existence of evil in general, and the reality of the Holocaust in particular. The argument was presented as a rhetorical question: "How is it possible to

---

8. Rabbi J.B. Soloveitchik, *Fate and Destiny: From the Holocaust to the State of Israel*, p. 4

9. Ibid., pp. 4-5

believe in God after what happened in the Holocaust?" From a Jewish perspective the answer to this question can be stated as follows: If you perceive the reality "under the sun" as ultimate, absolute reality, as the secular approach views it, then one has no choice but to recognize evil as a necessary and inseparable part of the world. Also with the partial view – "under the sun" – of man who is finite but believes in God, the absolute good and absolute justice in creation are not revealed. However, in contrast to the secular approach, which denies any reality beyond earthly life "under the sun", the believer is aware of the partial, temporary and finite nature of his physical reality. For him, the reality that is beyond life under the sun is no less real than his physical reality. Absolute good and justice are part of his faith, a faith that has performed wonders throughout the history of our nation, a history paved with suffering and death in sanctification of God's name. With this faith in absolute divine justice, and in the fact that evil is the heritage of a temporary, partial reality, our forefathers have found peace, hope and strength.

3. The Meaning of Life – a Connection to God

The Living God, in the Hebraic faith, is indeed the beginning and end of everything. Without Him, there is no life, no hope, no meaning; with Him in love and obedience to Him life is transfigured and begins to assume the quality and dimensions which belong to it in the order of creation.

Will Herberg, *Judaism and Modern Man*, p. 83

Now we will continue with the discussion of the meaning of life. It should be emphasized that this is one of the most important subjects in a discussion of the secular approach.

Concepts such as purpose and meaning do not belong at all to the world under the sun, which, according to the secular worldview, is governed solely by the forces of nature, and this is not dependent on the level of our knowledge of the laws that govern it. These concepts cannot be included in the framework of scientific thought, which deals with the laws of nature and their application.

When we talk about the meaning of life and the goals that we set for ourselves according to our understanding of it, we base these on the assumption that we are free to realize our goals, subject, of course, to the limitations of reality. We assume that human beings have free will. The concept of free will can also not be defined scientifically, since it does not belong to the realm of science. In Chapter Two, section 5, we saw that there are two kinds of causation that are entirely different in terms of their nature and their source: scientific causation and the causation that is connected with free will. This can be illustrated by a car travelling on a road, whose movement is carried out not only in accordance with the laws of nature – scientific causation – but its route is determined ultimately by the decisions of the driver – his choices. Similarly, man's life is composed of innumerable choices in his achievement of his goals, without breaching the laws of nature. This can only be because the physical world is open to man's choices (see Chapter Two, section 6).

In the first section we saw that from a secular perspective it is man, and only man, who gives life meaning, and we also saw how absurd and arbitrary this principle is. If it is impossible to determine rationally and objectively which values are preferable – liberal western values or those of the Nazis – then this means that all values are relative and arbitrary and life has no meaning.

In fact, the problem with the secular approach starts at an earlier point. In Chapter Four, sections 5 and 6, we saw that according to a consistent analysis of the secular approach a creature that is endowed with free will and creativity cannot be created by a purely materialistic process, such as evolution, without divine providence. It is worth reminding ourselves of what Einstein said, which we quoted in Chapter Two, section 5: "...there are no nonphysical elements in the causal system of the processes of nature. In this sense, there is no room for 'free will' within the framework of scientific thought." Without free will, life also has no meaning, since man who does not have free will cannot determine his goals and realize them.

We can conclude that the search for the meaning of life – according to the secular agenda – cannot bring any absolute or relative results. The deeper we search for meaning, the more we realize the futility of the endeavor. Secular thinking is not compatible with the existence of a universal and objective meaning of life.

Now let us turn to the subject of the meaning of life from a Jewish-religious perspective. I do not think that we are capable of grasping the full meaning of the life of man; this is only possible with the infinite perspective of the Creator. However, our inability to fully grasp the meaning of life does not release us from the obligation to search for the unique meaning of each person's life. It is important to comprehend, even partially, the meaning of life, but it is no less important to define the goals that derive from it and to realize those goals.

It is impossible to define once and for all the meaning of man's life in general. Each person strives to discover the meaning of his own life. While it is true that there are tasks and commandments that each of us is obligated to fulfill, this is not sufficient to define the meaning of man's life. It is just a common framework for everyone. Without detracting from the importance of the commandments, they are only a general frame for the life's purpose, and every individual must search for his own special mission. It would seem that this is an impossible task, but in fact it is a *creative* one. The meaning of my life, what I must do in this world, what my unique purpose is – these are not things that can be grasped and understood simply by logic or by studying books. Neither of these is sufficient. As with every creative act, more is needed – creativity is not achieved through study and logic. And not only comprehending the meaning of life, but also life itself must be a creative process. This is the important message that Judaism brought to the world.

Rabbi Soloveitchik writes in his book, *Halakhic Man*: "When man, the crowning glory of the cosmos, approaches the world, he finds his task at hand – the task of creation... the creature is commanded to become a partner with the Creator in the renewal of the cosmos" (*Halakhic Man*, p. 105). And: "The most fundamental principle of all is that man must create himself. It is this idea that Judaism introduced into the world" (Ibid. p. 109). "The peak of religious ethical perfection to which Judaism aspires is man as creator" (Ibid. p. 101).

The life of man is full of routine; we perform countless small, repetitive acts on a daily, and yearly, basis. We cannot imagine life without routine and habit. But man only fulfills his role if throughout his life he brings to the world new things that did not exist before him – if he creates – but this still does not define the meaning of his life. There are people who dedicate their entire lives to a creative field such as science or the arts. They "serve" science or the arts, and they see this service as their purpose and the meaning of their lives. In general, from the rationalist-secular viewpoint the meaning of a person's life is in the attainment of everything that he needs materially, and in creative activity that is held in high regard by his children, his family, his community and his nation. This gives him a sense of self-worth and meaning, and makes him fulfilled. In order that there should be meaning to his life man needs to know that he and his actions are important to people whose opinion he values. But why is this so important, since they too are transient beings? These are not new ideas. Three thousand years ago King Solomon described the folly of life "under the sun":

> "The words of Kohelet, the son of David, king in Jerusalem. Vanity of vanities, says Kohelet; vanity of vanities, all is vanity. What profit has man of all his labor wherein he labors under the sun? One generation passes away, and another generation comes; and the earth abides for ever." (Ecclesiastes 1:1-4)

> "I have seen all the works that are done under the sun; and, behold, all is vanity and a striving after wind. That which is crooked cannot be made straight; and that which is wanting cannot be numbered. I spoke with my own heart, saying: 'Lo, I have gotten great wisdom, more also than all that were before me over Jerusalem'; yea, my heart has had great experience of wisdom and knowledge. And I applied my heart to know wisdom, and to know madness and folly – I perceived that this also was a striving after wind." (Ibid. 1:14-17)

> "For of the wise man, even as of the fool, there is no remembrance for ever; seeing that in the days to come all will long ago have been forgotten. And how must the wise man die even as the fool! So I hated life; because the work that is wrought under the sun was grievous unto me; for all is vanity and a striving after wind." (Ibid. 2:16-17)

From a Jewish-religious perspective anything that does not have a connection to God does not have eternal, absolute meaning. Life goals can only have true meaning, meaning that is not transitory, if they have a connection with God. Without God there is no hope and there is no life; with Him – through love and obedience to Him – life gains quality and dimension as a creation of God. Man was created as God's partner in the completion of the world, *and the creative realization of this purpose is the meaning of his life.*

But the following questions arise here: What does this general approach give *me*? How can *I* understand the meaning of *my own life* from the above approach? The answer is that nowhere is the meaning of my own personal life written down, and nowhere are the objectives of my life that fit the above definition formulated. *The understanding of the meaning of my own life is a task no less creative than the realization of the objectives of life itself.* Here we see the importance of Judaism as a way of life: Jewish life is not just about the fulfillment of the commandments, but also about the study of Torah – the continuous study from the start of life until the end, which helps us familiarize ourselves with the paths of life. Great efforts and creativity are required for us to understand our place in the world and to discover the ends appropriate to the meaning of life of those who cling to God. The very aspiration to understand my place in the world and the purpose of my life itself contributes to my life's meaning.

In other places above, and in particular in Chapter Three, section 4, we discussed the idea of the openness of man's soul to God. Man has an active role in the creation of a connection between himself and God – he must continuously direct all his thoughts towards Him: "I have set the Lord always before me; surely He is at my right hand, I shall not be moved" (Psalms 16:8). A connection with God, the desire to reach Him and cling to Him, and actions that realize the holiness in man's life give it meaning. Without the dimension of holiness life loses the meaning that it has, that distinguishes it from that of all the other animals. Without holiness, life becomes life "under the sun" which is no different from the life of an animal: "For that which befalls the sons of men befalls beasts;

even one thing befalls them both. As the one dies, so dies the other. Yes, they have all one breath, so that man has no pre-eminence over a beast; for all is vanity" (Ecclesiastes 3:19).

According to the secular approach, man's life has no place for God, and hence it also has no place for holiness. Furthermore, a consistent secular approach would claim that life itself has no holiness. In the first section we brought a quote from a famous biologist that we cannot "regard all human life as sacred". Man himself defines the purpose and goals of life. And in the absence of meaning for anything other than life, secular man attributes absolute meaning to the existence of his intelligence and to the results of his intellect. In contrast, Judaism ascribes absoluteness solely to God.

According to the God-free secular approach, there is no uniform, absolute meaning that is common to all human beings. Absolute meaning is attributed to a superior race, or to class struggle, to the rights of man, to war for freedom or to terrorism – all of these are examples of the "sacred" goals of different groups of human beings. From a Jewish-religious perspective, these are different incarnations of idolatry. I will explain what I mean. In Judaism, idolatry is one of the most grievous sins and is the source of bad deeds. To comprehend this it is important to understand precisely what idolatry is. Idolatry is not only worshipping and bowing down to idols and statues. If it were, then it would be of no relevance to modern times. *Idolatry is the attribution of absoluteness to something that is only relative; it is the absolute sanctification of something that is devoid of sanctity and absoluteness.* The object of idolatry can even be something good. But since it is only partially and relatively good, it does not have the value of absolute goodness. Idolatry distracts a person from the worship of God. Modern, secular man attributes God's qualities to nature and its laws, and thus loses the connection with God, a connection that distinguishes him from the entire animal kingdom – "and man has no pre-eminence over a beast". We can conclude by saying that *secularism is the idolatry of our times, and this is the root of the sins of modern man.*

The main conclusion of this chapter is that the secular approach does not provide meaning either to history or to the life of man, and that the meaning of man's life and the development of history both belong to the divine realm, and are connected to it. From the point of view of the secular thinker, our world is a closed system that develops independently but is not capable of providing lawfulness and meaning for itself. Hence, I have stressed numerous times that from a secular perspective it is impossible to distinguish between the different approaches to human morality, for example between communism and western liberalism, since there are no criteria that are external to the world, to humankind, and to man. On the other hand, according to the Jewish-religious view, it is possible to distinguish between the various ethical systems based on how close they are to the sources in the Jewish writings. Thus, western humanism is definitely preferable to the various totalitarian ideologies, as it contains various elements of religious morality. In contrast, a philosopher who adheres to a consistent secular approach tends to remove the religious elements in his worldview. Earlier, I quoted a famous biologist who claimed that we must rid ourselves of the concept of the sanctity of life. According to Jacques Monod, another famous biologist, all development of life is the result of chance, and hence we must rid ourselves of the western humanistic legacy: "For their moral bases the 'liberal' societies of the West still teach – or pay lip service to – a disgusting farrago of Judeo-Christian religiosity, scientistic progressism, belief in the 'natural' rights of man..."[1]. Hence, while a philosopher subscribes to the belief that chance is the source of life and its development, he cannot avoid the conclusion that our lives have no meaning.

---

1. Chance and Necessity, p. 171

EPILOGUE: THE GAPS OF SECULARISM

A World Open to God and Man's Will versus a Closed, Imaginary World that Develops on Its Own

Throughout the book we have highlighted the gaps in the secular approach to understanding the world and man's place within it. Now we will try to show that the existence of these gaps refutes the secular approach to describing and understanding the world in general. We started by looking at the phenomenon of man, which is, in my opinion, the greatest challenge to the secular worldview. Now we will conclude, on a very general level, the picture of the development of the world, which led to the creation of man – the crowning glory of creation. The diagram below shows the development of the world, indicating the elements that the secular approach is incapable of dealing with – the gaps in the secular approach.

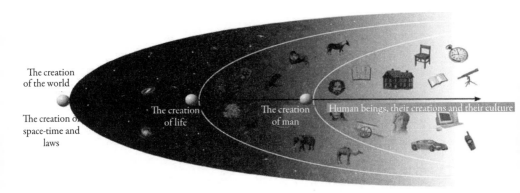

The creation of the world

The creation of space-time and laws

The creation of life

The creation of man

Human beings, their creations and their culture

According to both the Torah and science, there were three major creations in the development of the world: the creation of the world itself, the creation of life, and the creation of man. These are marked in the diagram with gray spheres. Let us take a look at these events and at the development of the world, life and man, which took place after each one.

A very long time ago (fifteen-and-a-half billion years ago, according to scientific estimates) our world was created. According to the general theory of relativity, in the beginning the whole universe was concentrated in one very tiny volume – in one point. From that moment it began to expand until it reached its present size. During the expansion, stars and star clusters – galaxies – were formed. It should be noted that a star is not simply a lump of matter, but a physical structure that creates heat and light over billions of years, a thermo-nuclear furnace. One of the stars that was formed during the expansion and development of the universe was our sun. Over the course of time various planets were formed around the sun, amongst them, planet Earth.

Approximately three-and-a-half billions years ago (according to scientific estimates) the second major creation took place – the creation of life. The first living being was created on Earth, and the era of life began. Life spread out and many new species were created, and a relatively short time ago (tens of thousands of years ago) the third major creation occurred: a completely new creature was formed that was different from anything in the world up to that point – man.

Man was created as the result of a long and complex process. Man, and life in general, could not have been created at the early stages of the development of the world. He could not have been created prior to the creation of the air that he breathes, or without water or food from his environment. He needs heat, and he can only exist within a fairly limited temperature range. Hence, for the existence of man, the solar system is needed. One might think that this was sufficient – man is capable of existing in a relatively small world, the size of the solar system, and the huge spaces of our universe do not affect him at all. However, modern science shows us otherwise: Only a very large universe such as ours can make the existence of man possible. In order to produce the basic elements of life – carbon, nitrogen, oxygen and phosphorus – the simple elements, hydrogen and helium, which were present at the initial stage of the Big Bang, needed "to ripen" by way of thermo-nuclear reactions that took place among the stars. When stars are extinguished they explode (supernovae) and vital elements scatter in space and come together to form planets and eventually to form us. This planetary "alchemy" requires a period of more than ten billion years.

"[F]or there to be enough time to construct the constituents of living beings, the Universe must be at least ten billion years old and therefore, as a consequence of its expansion, at least ten billion light years in extent. We should not be surprised to observe that the Universe is so large. No astronomer could exist in one that was significantly smaller. The Universe needs to be as big as it is in order to evolve just a single carbon-based life form." (J.D. Barrow & F.J. Tipler, *The Anthropic Cosmological Principle*, p. 3)

After the creation of man, the era of human history began. Each person is a complete spiritual world. The history of humankind is characterized by great creativity. Every creation is an appearance of something new that did not exist before, and which does not derive from anything that existed up until that point. The creativity of man is connected to a new phenomenon that entered the world with his creation – his free will.

These are, in completely general terms, the characteristics of the world during its development. In this section we are going to conclude our discussion about the poverty of secularism. The dividing line between the secular approach and the religious approach lies in their understanding of the process of the creation and development of the world described above. There is no difference in the *description* of this process by the secular and religious views (perhaps there is a difference in their treatment of the age of the world, whether it is finite or infinite, but here even the secular view is not uniform). The difference lies in the *understanding* and *explanation* of the structure of the world and the processes of its development. The key difference is in the answer to the following question: *Is the world and everything in it, including human beings, a closed system that develops solely in accordance with internal forces (the laws of nature) or is the existence of the world and its development dependent on an external entity, God according to religious belief?* The message of this book, as we shall soon conclude, is unequivocal: It is impossible to understand and explain the creation and the development of the world, which led to the appearance of man, as the result of internal forces alone, namely, as the result of the action of the laws of nature on the matter in the world. According to the secular view, the origin and source of the development of the world is matter. Hence, according to the secular approach, the world, its development and everything in it can be explained solely using scientific tools. We claim categorically that the view that states that it is possible to understand and explain the world solely using scientific tools is incorrect. Our world is not a closed system that develops solely via internal forces.

We shall summarize the processes of the development of the world in a systematic way, starting from its creation.

The creation of the world: The creation of the world is the greatest mystery from a secular perspective. In fact, it is not actually the creation of the world itself that is difficult (since from a secular perspective it is possible to deny its existence), but that which accompanies it – space and time and the law and order in the world. From a secular perspective there is no explanation, and nor can there be, for the existence of order in the world. In Chapter Three, section 2, we quoted Albert Einstein, saying that the scientific enterprise – the possibility of explaining the world by science – is a miracle in itself: "Now, a priori, one should, after all, expect a chaotic world... *the success of such an enterprise does suppose a high degree of order in the objective world,* which one had no justification whatever to expect a priori. Here lies the sense of 'wonder' which increases even more with the development of our knowledge." Einstein emphasizes that the development of science not only does not decrease the miracle but "increases [it] even more". If the order is not imposed on the world from the outside, it is impossible to explain its existence.

From a secular perspective, this is not the only mystery related to the creation of the world. The uniformity of the laws of nature constitutes a "gap" in the fabric of secular thought. In Chapter Two, section 3 we quoted Karl Popper stating that it is impossible to understand why the laws of nature are identical everywhere in the world: "The structural homogeneity of the world seems to resist any 'deeper' explanation: it remains a mystery." But the mystery is solved when we take into account that there is an external source for the laws of nature – God, who imposes them on the world.

Recently there have been many discussions in the scientific literature about the compatibility of the laws of nature to life – the anthropic principle. Of all the combinations of possible laws of nature, only certain laws, that are within a very limited range, are compatible with life. That is, the laws of nature in our world are extremely delicately fine-tuned to the formation of life, and it is possible to imagine that at the moment of the creation of the world the formation of life in the future was already planned. The anthropic principle, the compatibility of the laws of nature to life, remains a mystery, a *gap* in the fabric of secular thought. It does not prove the existence of the creator, but on the other hand it is impossible to ignore it. It adds another rock to the solid foundation of belief in God.

In Chapter Two, section 6 it became apparent that there is another condition that the laws of nature must fulfill: compatibility with the existence of man's free will. Again it is important to stress that the issues related to the creation of the laws of nature, to their existence and their nature, do not fall within the realm of secular thought. The very existence of the laws of nature is a mystery from a secular perspective.

Science: It is interesting that science and its achievements are considered to be the stronghold of the secular approach. The irony is that a consistent philosophical analysis leads to the conclusion that in the framework of secular thought the very existence of science is an insoluble problem; the phenomenon of science is a miracle for which there is no rational explanation. This is an additional "gap" or weakness in the fabric of secular thought.

From a secular perspective, the fact that we are capable of knowing the world is a mystery. In the eyes of the secular thinker, knowledge of the world in general, and of the laws of nature in particular, are a riddle and a mystery. Karl Popper, who was a staunch believer in the secular approach wrote: "The phenomenon of human knowledge is no doubt the greatest miracle in our universe." Albert Einstein expressed a similar view: "The eternal mystery of the world is its comprehensibility... The fact that it is comprehensible is a miracle." It is impossible to understand the phenomenon of scientific discovery using the tools of secular thought. In the closed imaginary world of the secular thinker there is no room for the mighty enterprise of science. Only when the openness of the world to God and His providence are taken into account is it possible to understand the phenomenon of science.

The development of the world until the creation of life. After the creation of the world and its laws, the development of the world began. The world expanded and became bigger and bigger; stars, galaxies and planets were formed, amongst them, planet Earth. This process took place in accordance with the laws of nature which were created together with the world. From a religious point of view, the development of the world takes place under divine supervision, one of the tools of which is the laws of nature. A study of the process of the development of the world up to (but not including) the formation of life does not give a definitive answer to the question of whether the laws of nature are sufficient for a description of the formation of the stars and galaxies. In the absence of a definitive answer to this question, it is possible to assume that the laws of nature are the main (and perhaps the only) tool of providence at this stage, which does not include the creation of the world and the creation of life, and hence it can be described scientifically. One can say that *only with regard to this stage* is it possible that there is no contradiction between the religious view and the secular view. However, the process of the creation of the world and its development up to the creation of life cannot be fully understood from a secular perspective. It includes mysteries that are impossible to comprehend or explain from this point of view. Hence, without any connection to the reasonableness of the explanation of the process of the development of the world from the creation of life and onwards, this first stage is an impenetrable barrier to the secular view. But as we have seen throughout the book, creation and the development of life and humanity are barriers that are no less impenetrable for the secular view. It is on this subject that we shall now concentrate.

We see that up until the beginning of the era of life there was a fairly prolonged period of the creation of the world and its development. When people claim that the theory of evolution explains the development of life and the appearance of man on Earth, it appears that they are assuming that the stage up to the creation of life can be explained solely using scientific tools and what was not understood and explained prior to Darwin was how life developed and man appeared on Earth. But presenting the matter in this way does not reflect reality at all. As we saw above, for the development and formation of the vital material elements of life a process was required that included the *creation of the world* along with *the creation of the appropriate laws of nature* (the anthropic principle), the source of which is external to the world, and their uniformity is an indication of this. As we saw, there is no scientific treatment of these things, and nor can there be, since they do not belong to the field of science. Hence, we come to the conclusion that the history of the world prior to evolution, in its entirety, does not belong to science – it has elements that do not belong to science at all.

The creation of life and its development. Three-and-a-half billion years ago (according to scientific estimates) the second major creation took place: the creation of life. In the diagram at the start of the section this creation is marked by a gray sphere, similarly to the creation of the world, and what they have in common is the appearance of something completely new that is unlike anything that existed before it. The creation of the first living creature brought to the world an entity of a kind that was different from that which existed before – the era of life had begun. The life expanded, and many new species were created. Likewise, the world started to expand after its creation. But this is where the similarity ends. The expansion of the world can be studied using scientific means, and there are scientific theories that describe the development of the physical world. But as we saw in Chapter Four, there is no scientific theory of the development of life on Earth, and nor can there be one. The reason for this is quite simple: the development of life is a sequence of events which are not connected by any definitive causal link, and (according to the scientific approach) it is random factors that determine the different stages of development. In other words, there is no law of evolution. And if there is no law, then it is impossible to build a scientific theory of the development of life; no hypotheses regarding the evolution of life on Earth have scientific status. In Chapter Four, section 4, we quoted Karl Popper, saying: "There exists no law of evolution, only the historical fact that plants and animals change, or more precisely, that they have changed. The idea of a law which determines the direction and the character of evolution is *a typical nineteenth-century mistake, arising out of the general tendency to ascribe to the*

'Natural Law' the functions traditionally ascribed to God".

Despite the commonly held notion, held by laymen, scientists and philosophers alike, that the development of life can be explained using scientific tools, consistent analysis and inquiry lead to the unequivocal conclusion: there is no scientific theory of the evolution of life, and nor can there be. This is a very significant weakness in the fabric of secular thought, because it attributes supreme importance to the possibility of explaining the evolution of life using scientific tools. But one can respond to the claim about the lack of a scientific theory that even if there is no scientific theory of evolution, it is reasonable to assume that the natural selection mechanism is the cause of evolution. We considered this argument in Chapter Four, sections 5 and 6, and we came to the unequivocal conclusion: The materialist-evolutionary process is not capable of leading to the creation of man, who is endowed with free will and creativity.

Some more remarks about creativity. In Chapter Three, section 4 we mentioned that there is a strong connection between the phenomenon of creation and divine providence. A true creation is always something new that does not derive from anything that existed in the world. It is something that is not from our world, but from outside of it, as can be deduced from the concept of "creation *ex nihilo*" – *nihilo* means that it does not belong to our world. A true creation involves providence, divine involvement. The creation of law and order in the world also belongs to divine creation – the setting of the stage, the fixed framework of divine action. On the other hand, from a secular perspective the existence of creativity in the world is a mystery. In Chapter Three, section 4 we quoted Popper, saying: "I would even suggest that the greatest riddle of cosmology may well be neither the original big bang, nor

the problem why there is something rather than nothing...
but that the universe is, in a sense, creative: that it created
life, and from it mind - our consciousness - which illuminates
the universe, and which is creative in its turn..." However,
only from the perspective of a secular thinker, who does not
recognize a creator who presides over the world, can one talk
about the 'creativity of the world'. From the secular point of
view, the world is closed to God's intervention, and if creation
does exist, it must be the result of factors within the world, of
the forces of nature, and it is therefore a mystery – since the
laws of nature are not creative.

From a Jewish-religious perspective, the world is open to
divine providence and the process of the development of life
is accompanied by many divine creations. In fact, every new
species is a divine creation. But these creations constitute
"gaps" in the secular view, as we have stated that the theory
of evolution does not provide an explanation for them, despite
the claims of the followers of Darwinism.

The creation of man and the development of humankind.
This is the third major creation, after the creation of the world
and the creation of life. In the routine of our daily lives we have
become accustomed to the existence of man and we do not
see any wonder in his existence. But, in fact, the phenomenon
of man is the greatest miracle in the world, greater than all the
miracles that we know of, but in order to appreciate it we must
get away from the routine way of thinking that views what we
see all the time as self-evident. Furthermore, great wisdom
and knowledge are required to discern the wondrous side
in something "ordinary". I brought the words of the Psalmist
above: "How great are your deeds, Lord, exceedingly profound
are your thoughts. A simple man cannot know, nor can a fool
understand this." (Psalms 92:6-7)

With the creation of man came the start of a new era – the era of man – and human history began. This new creature has qualities and characteristics that no creature before him has possessed. He has a soul, self-consciousness, free will, creativity and communication with God. A consistent secular analysis leads to the unfeasibility of these characteristics. A consistent secular thinker must deny the existence of the soul and of the possibility of communication with God, and must recognize his inability to understand other characteristics. Thus Karl Popper writes in his book *The Self and Its Brain* (which he wrote together with John Eccles): "The emergence of full consciousness, capable of self-reflection, which seems to be linked to the human brain and to the descriptive function of language, is indeed one of the greatest of miracles."[2]

It should be said that the recognition of the uniqueness of man is not a recent discovery. Eight hundred years ago, Maimonides wrote about the magnificence of man's intellectual achievement, and explained it by man's connection to God:

Now man possesses as his proprium something in him that is very strange as it is not found in anything else that exists under the sphere of the moon, namely, intellectual apprehension. In the exercise of this, no sense, no part of the body, none of the extremities are used; and therefore this apprehension was likened unto the apprehension of the deity, which does not require an instrument, although in reality it is not like the latter apprehension, but only appears so to the first stirrings of opinion. It was because of this something, I mean *because of the divine intellect conjoined with man*, that it is said of the latter that he is in the image of God and in His likeness...[3]

---

2. K.R. Popper and J.C. Eccles, *The Self and Its Brain*, p. 129

3. *Guide of the Perplexed*, 1:1

We have reached the conclusion that the materialistic-evolutionary process is not capable of leading to the creation of man who is endowed with free will. From here it follows that man's spiritual characteristics are not within the grasp of secular philosophy. The secular position, if one follows it consistently to its end, leads to the conclusion that there is no soul, there is no consciousness, there is no free will and there is no creativity. And if the secular thinker nonetheless believes in the existence of certain spiritual characteristics, then he must conclude that they are a mystery that cannot be understood from the secular point of view. We quoted Popper above, that the appearance of self-consciousness is a miracle, and that the phenomenon of creativity is the greatest of mysteries. The existence of free will is also not compatible with the secular approach, as Einstein states (see Chapter Two, section 5): "In this sense, there is no room for 'free will' in the framework of scientific thought..."

The secular approach starts with the assumption that everything in the world, including human beings, is the sole result of the operation of the laws of nature. Therefore, the following question arises: What meaning, if any, can be attributed to the life of man, to human society and to history, in the framework of the secular approach? Here we must make a clear distinction between what any particular secular philosopher claims, and what follows from a consistent analysis of the secular theses. Despite the claims of philosophers such as Hegel, Marx, Engels and their followers, about the existence of internal lawfulness latent in history, Karl Popper's well-argued analysis leads to the definitive conclusion that there is no internal order in the processes of history. From the same analysis it follows that if there is no internal order or lawfulness in history, then human history also has no meaning. We must recognize the fact that the lack of meaning in the process of history is the conclusion that follows from the theses of the secular approach.

Now let us turn to the most important subject from man's point of view – the meaning of life. We have mentioned that the secular approach regarding man conceals a deep internal contradiction. On the one hand man is a product of nature and therefore lacks a soul and spiritual characteristics, while on the other hand he is at the center of the world and determines the meaning of his own life and that of others. In the absence of meaning for anything other than man, secular man attributes absolute meaning to his own intellect and to values that derive from his intellect. In contrast, Judaism attributes the quality of absoluteness to God alone.

According to the godless secular approach, there is no uniform and absolute meaning for all human beings. Absolute meaning is attributed to a variety of goals that are considered "sacred" in the eyes of particular groups of people. In fact, this approach is a kind of idolatry, one of the most grievous sins according to Judaism. To understand this claim it is important to understand precisely what idolatry is. Idolatry is not only worshipping and bowing down to idols and statues. If it were, then it would be of no relevance to modern times. *Idolatry is the attribution of absoluteness to something that is only relative; it is the absolute sanctification of something that is devoid of sanctity and absoluteness.* Nothing other than God has absolutely goodness or absolute value. Idolatry distracts a person from the worship of God. Modern, secular man attributes God's qualities to nature and its laws, and thus loses the connection with God, a connection that distinguishes him from the entire animal kingdom – and "man has no pre-eminence over a beast". We can conclude by saying that *secularism is the idolatry of our times, and this is the root of the sins of modern man.*

The statement that idolatry distracts a person from the worship of God has no place in secular language, and it does not have an effect on the secular interlocutor. He does not worship God in the first place. However, an important point in the discussion with the secular man follows directly from what we have said – on the basis of the secular theses alone, it is impossible to reach an understanding of the world and man. The secular approach cannot form a basis for any of the human intellectual fields: *science, philosophy, ethics, cosmogony (the study of the formation of the universe), cosmology, and the study of the development of life and humanity.* The weaknesses of secularism, which we have discussed above, prevent us from building a solid foundation in any of these fields.

In the first chapter we posited the phenomenon of man as the ultimate challenge for the various secular approaches. The challenge is in understanding man's coming into being on Earth. We asked ourselves: *How could man have been created – a creature so complex, so sophisticated and wondrous, which belongs both to the world of the spirit and to the world of matter?* We saw that this question has two possible answers. The first is compatible with both common sense and our accumulated experience, and states that, as with all the creations, even the simplest amongst them, there must be a creator – so it is with man, the most complex creature known to us; the second answer is compatible with the secular worldview, and states that man was created from nature, or to be more precise, nature itself created man, and science proves this. Throughout the book we have seen the incredible unreasonableness of this view, for which there is no reasoning, either scientific or logical. On the contrary, we have brought clear proofs for the impossibility of the creation of man by nature.

We often hear the following rhetorical question: How can an educated person of the twenty-first century believe in things such as divine providence? We can answer this question unequivocally: A truly educated person cannot believe that nature created its own laws, life and man himself. Only as a result of sheer ignorance is it possible to believe such stories.

Appendix: A Response to Dawkins' The God Delusion

This book actually already contains a clear and detailed response to the extreme physicalist worldview presented in Dawkins' book, *The God Delusion*[1]. I could have simply made these comments in the body of the book. However, Dawkins' book, in which he misleads a huge audience of readers by his mistaken assertion that there is a scientific rationale to his atheistic view, has become a bestseller. Therefore, I have decided to respond to the principal claims presented in his book. My response to each of Dawkins' claims consists of a concise argument and a short summary at the end.

1. "The 'God Hypothesis' is a scientific hypothesis about the universe, which should be analyzed as skeptically as any other." (p. 2)

Dawkins opens his book with this statement, and continues throughout the book with a stubborn and uncompromising use of the scientific pretext. For example: "*The presence or absence of a creative super-intelligence is unequivocally a scientific question, even if it is not in practice – or not yet – a decided one.*" (p. 82)

Therefore, we should briefly review the nature of science, and consider what differentiates it from other enterprises of human thought, such as philosophy. In Chapter Three, section 2 we learned that scientific theories are hypotheses (guesses) which can be tested by experiment. The experi-

---

1. Dawkins, Richard, *The God Delusion*, Houghton Mifflin Co., Boston, 2008

ments can corroborate the scientific theory, reinforce its validity in its area of application or refute it, but they cannot verify it – they cannot prove it to be true. At the foundation of science lies the understanding, or the belief (we shall discuss this further in due course) that laws of nature exist, and that scientific theories – scientific hypotheses – are an approximation to these laws of nature.

I would like to add a few words about the concept of truth. Alfred Tarski, a twentieth century logician, came to some important conclusions regarding the existence of truth. Truth exists and can be defined, but in general it is impossible to prove it, to verify it, though it can be corroborated. A scientific theory does not prove that there is a law of nature; however the existence of such a law is a metaphysical truth that lies at the foundation of science. I should point out that there is a crucial difference between science and metaphysics. A scientific theory can be refuted, while a metaphysical statement cannot be refuted (nor can it be verified). We have Karl Popper to thank for providing a clear distinction between scientific and metaphysical claims.

The goal of science is to investigate the lawfulness in nature, the development of the objects of nature to the extent that it is determined by the laws of nature (not all developments in nature are determined by the laws – there are also random processes that are not determined by any law). It is also important to understand that scientific study is not absolute – scientific theories have the status of guesses, hypotheses, which can be corroborated or refuted, but which cannot be verified.

Given this, the absurdity of the claim that the existence of God is a scientific hypothesis and that it can be tested just like any other scientific hypothesis, is blatantly clear. This assertion is repeated several times in Dawkins' book, and is a foundation of his atheistic viewpoint. But God is not part of nature, whose existence can be tested by scientific experiment; He is above nature. To say that the hypothesis regarding the existence of

God is a scientific hypothesis about the world is like saying that God is a part of nature and obeys its laws. This is nothing but a paganistic view that deifies nature, and, in fact, it is this kind of deity against which Dawkins is arguing, rather than the actual God. As Alister McGrath notes in relation to Dawkins' position regarding religion: "Having set up his straw man, Dawkins knocks it down."[2]

Let us summarize: *The claim that the "God Hypothesis" is a scientific hypothesis lies at the foundation of Dawkins' atheistic analysis. There is no rational basis to the claim that the hypothesis that God exists is a kind of scientific hypothesis, and it arises from a complete misunderstanding both of the scientific approach and of the concept of God. Hence the atheistic claims that seemingly derive from this claim have no validity whatsoever.*

2. *"Natural selection not only explains the whole of life; it also raises our consciousness to the power of science to explain how organized complexity can emerge from simple beginnings without any deliberate guidance." (p. 141)*

Dawkins is convinced of, and tries to plant in the readers' minds, his view that the Darwinist theory of natural selection is a scientific theory that explains the evolution of life, and that in light of its success one can be certain that in the future science will also explain the appearance of order in the inanimate world. We emphasized above that a scientific theory is a hypothesis that can be tested by experiment, but we do not have direct experimental access to the history of Earth. This was Karl Popper's argument that the Darwinist account is not a scientific theory but a metaphysical belief.

However, my main argument here is that any natural, physical process can be studied using scientific tools only if there is a law of nature that

---

2. McGrath, Alister, *Dawkins' God: Genes, Memes, and the Meaning of Life*, Blackwell Publish., Oxford, 2007, p. 86

determines that process. Even though one might be under the impression that the laws of nature determine all natural processes, this is not, in fact, the case. In nature there are random processes that are not determined by any law. The movement of a single quantum particle, in general, is not determined by any law – the statistical law only relates to a large group of quantum objects. The development of life according to the theory of natural selection is also not determined by any law, as it has a random element related to mutations. This element is vital – without it, according to the Darwinist account, evolution would not exist at all. A statistical theory cannot help here (and nor does such a theory exist), since there is only one world, and the evolutionary process that takes place in it is also a singular thing. In Chapter Four, section 4 I quoted important biologists who testified to the absence of a law of evolution. And Karl Popper wrote:

> There exists no law of evolution, only the historical fact that plants and animals change, or more precisely, that they have changed. The idea of a law which determines the direction and the character of evolution is *a typical nineteenth-century mistake, arising out of the general tendency to ascribe to the 'Natural Law' the functions traditionally ascribed to God.*

Together with the arguments of other thinkers, we have come to the conclusion that there is no law of evolution and there is no scientific theory that describes the evolution of life on Earth. Without a doubt, the processes of natural selection lead to an improvement of the functioning of individuals of existing species. But there are no empirical proofs for the creation of new species by natural selection. Darwinism simply proposes a particular suggestion, a particular hypothesis, of the essence of evolution. We have seen that all scientific theories are hypotheses, but not every hypothesis is a scientific theory. The latter must meet certain criteria, which the Darwinist account does not meet. Hence, the Darwinist account is a metaphysical belief about the essence of the evolution of life. At this point we could make do with saying, along with Alister McGrath: "We may *believe* that Darwinism is right, but we cannot *know* that this is so."[3]

However, it is important to add the following. According to Dawkins' materialist view, the world of matter is closed and there is no external power that influences its development. Hence, this kind of development is capable of "creating" things that are made purely from matter. According to this view, man is also a product of material evolution, of a perfectly materialistic process that is based on a combination of lawfulness and chance. But man is also endowed with unmistakably spiritual qualities such as free will, self-consciousness, emotions and the ability to create varied and diverse creations. In this book, in Chapter Four, section 6 in particular, we showed *the inability of a purely materialistic process such as natural selection to lead to man's spiritual qualities.* Of course, there is a metaphysical alternative which is to deny the existence of man's spiritual qualities, to say that they are only illusory, and to recognize that we, human beings, are nothing but meaningless *robots*. This is, in fact, the absurd metaphysical belief held by Dawkins, a belief that has no basis in reality. And this is obviously not a scientific view, as he claims.

To summarize: There is no argument regarding the existence of the evolution of life on Earth. The problem lies in understanding the process. *The Darwinist account is not a scientific theory – it is nothing but a metaphysical belief in the idea that the natural selection mechanism alone is capable of bringing about evolution. But this is not a reasonable belief, since a purely material process, without any external cause – such as God – is not capable of creating man's spiritual qualities, which constitute his very essence.*

---

3. Ibid. p. 107

3. *"Faith means blind trust, in the absence of evidence, even in the teeth of evidence..."*[4]

Dawkins presents faith as something meaningless, in contrast with science which provides tested and proven knowledge. Why should we believe in something that cannot be proven scientifically?

"But what, after all, is faith? It is a state of mind that leads people to believe something – it doesn't matter what – in the total absence of supporting evidence. If there were good supporting evidence, then faith would be superfluous, for the evidence would compel us to believe it anyway."[5]

And Dawkins adds:

"Faith is an evil precisely because it requires no justification and brooks no argument."[6]

Dawkins is referring here both to belief in God and other beliefs in general. We will now see that Dawkins' approach to faith is both incorrect and misleading.

In order to relate to Dawkins' position regarding different beliefs, let us ponder for a moment the essence of faith. Is it possible to distinguish between a more founded belief and a less founded belief? And what connection is there, if any, between faith and science? In fact, a study of the reciprocal relationship between science and faith will help us understand the essence of faith. It is important to understand that science is based on certain metaphysical foundations, which are derived neither from experience, nor logic, and which have the status of beliefs. One of these foundations is the belief that law and order prevail in the world, and this is actually the belief in a creator of the world who imposes them on it. I should stress that there is absolutely no possibility of proving the existence

---

4.   Dawkins, R. *The Selfish Gene*, Oxford University Press, 1989, p. 198

5.   Ibid. p. 330

6.   Dawkins, Richard, *The God Delusion*, p. 347

of the laws of nature; one can only believe in them. There is no proof that a law that seems to be tested and stable will remain that way in the future – we can only believe this. On the other hand, every scientific study is based on a belief in the order prevailing in the world, in the existence of the laws of nature. Einstein and Infeld stress this explicitly in their book, *The Evolution of Physics*. They write in the final section of the book: "[W] ithout the belief in the inner harmony of our world, there could be no science. This belief is and always will remain the fundamental motive for all scientific creation." The philosopher Alfred Whitehead also states that "...the restless modern search for increased accuracy of observation and for increased detailed explanation is based upon unquestioning faith in the reign of Law. Apart from such faith, the enterprise of science is foolish, hopeless."[7]

We, human beings, are not able to prove the existence of a law of nature, we can only believe in it. The scientific enterprise is based on this belief, and this is what is emphasized in the points we brought above. On the other hand, the belief in the existence of a law of nature is reinforced by the outstanding achievements of science. It is impossible to *prove* the existence of the law, but the fulfillment of innumerable predictions of scientific theories *corroborates* its existence. In this sentence, the difference between proof and corroboration is highlighted. We *believe* in the existence of the laws of nature, but we cannot *prove* that, on top of all the scientific predictions and their fulfillment, there exists an absolute law that will never change in the future. Because of this, Whitehead, Einstein and Infeld talk about belief. The fulfillment of the predictions of science corroborates and reinforces the belief that behind all these predictions there stands an absolute law. We might say that the belief in the existence of the laws of nature is a very well-founded belief.

This discussion concerns the existence of the laws of nature, but what

---

7. *Adventures of Ideas*, p. 135

about the existence of free will? According to Dawkins, all creatures, including man, act solely in accordance with the laws of physics.[8] Hence there is no room for free will, which, along with man's other spiritual qualities are simply an illusion. However, the belief in the existence of free will is also reinforced by innumerable predictions and their fulfillment. We cannot prove the existence of free will, just as we cannot prove the existence of the laws of nature, but man's ability to plan and to realize his plans reinforces his belief in free will. There is a basis for the belief in free will, just as there is a basis for the belief in the existence of a law of nature. Countless experiments and experiences reinforce both beliefs.

Now let us turn to belief in God, the belief that Dawkins singled out as the main object of his critique. It is well-known that it is impossible to prove or refute the existence of God. But the main conclusion of this book is that no enterprise of human thought is complete without taking God's existence into account. It is interesting that this was also the conclusion arrived at by James Clerk Maxwell: "I have looked into most philosophical systems, and I have seen that none will work without God."[9] In this book we have examined two contrasting worldviews – a world open to God and the wills of man, versus a closed, imaginary world that develops on its own – and we have shown the unfoundedness of the secular view, which is devoid of God. Without a doubt, this conclusion reinforces belief in a creator.

Just as at the foundation of scientific study lies the belief in the existence of law and order in nature, at the foundation of the existence of the world as a whole lies the belief in God. Dawkins, in his argument against opposing worldviews, quotes Martin Rees: "The pre-eminent mystery is why anything exists at all. What breathes life into the equations of physics,

8. "The *physical stance* always works in principle, because everything ultimately obeys the laws of physics." (*The God Delusion*, p. 211)

9. *The Life of James Clerk Maxwell*, p. 426

and actualized them in a real cosmos?"[10] We saw in Chapter Two, section 2, that the laws of nature – and the equations of physics that express them – have no meaning without God imposing them on nature. A world that develops without God sustaining it is not feasible – it is impossible to comprehend.

In the first paragraph of this appendix we noted that God, by his very nature, is above and beyond nature. If so, the divine spiritual reality does not belong to scientific study. The job of science is to study the processes that occur in nature, as determined by the laws of nature. However, as we noted above, not all natural processes behave in accordance with defined lawfulness. Also the material processes of the development of life are not determined solely by laws. The widely accepted notion, the view which is popular amongst many, including scientists, is that everything in the world, without exception, can be subject to scientific study and explanation. Dawkins, in his naivety, and ignoring the weighty philosophical arguments, takes this to the extreme and claims that God is the object of scientific study.[11] The absolute absurdity of such a view, that assumes that God is an entity that complies with the laws of nature, is blatantly clear.

Throughout his discussion about the existence of God, Dawkins completely ignores numerous testimonies of many people, in the past and the present, of their personal connection with God. Furthermore, in Chapter Three of this book we came to the conclusion that a scientific discovery is also a kind of divine revelation, without which the development of science would be impossible. From a secular perspective, the existence of science is a miracle, as Einstein put it: "The eternal mystery of the world is its comprehensibility... The fact that it is comprehensible is a miracle."

---

10. Rees, M., *Our Cosmic Habitat*, Weidenfeld & Nicolson, London, 2001

11. "The presence or absence of a creative super-intelligence is unequivocally a scientific question, even if it is not in practice – or not yet – a decided one." (*The God Delusion*, p. 82)

We can summarize as follows: *Belief in God lies at the foundation of the study of the world in which we live. Without it, (and we proved this in this book) we are not able to understand our world, how it was created and how it develops. Belief is not "blind faith" or "a bad thing", as Dawkins claims, but is the foundation of a consistent worldview.*

4. Constantly renewing creation

"...design is ultimately not cumulative and it therefore raises bigger questions than it answers..." *(p. 169)*

As far as Dawkins is concerned, divine design is a one-off event, in contrast with material evolution, which is operated by natural selection and takes place over time. Hence divine design is not capable of explaining the development of life, which the theory of natural selection, it seems, can explain. However, this is just another of Dawkins' misunderstandings, and seems to arise from his lack of knowledge of Jewish thought. I will now give a brief synopsis of the Jewish approach to this subject. The creation of the world is not only the founding event of the beginning of the world, but also of its continuous creation. This is the concept of the constantly renewing creation expressed in the words: "and in His goodness renews daily, perpetually, the work of creation". Our world was not created once at one particular point in time in the past, and since then simply exists on its own. Every day and each moment – "perpetually" – creation is renewed. This profound truth of the Jewish-religious worldview was hidden from Dawkins' field of vision. As we saw earlier in this book, it is impossible to explain the varied and diverse creations that appear as part of the development of the world, *ex nihilo*, without attributing them to divine providence that operates constantly, "daily, perpetually".

Dawkins understands that the theory of natural selection is not capable of providing an explanation for the process of the evolution of life in general.[12] There are events that cannot be explained through the natural selection mechanism, even with his most generous interpretation. Dawkins solves the problem by relating to these events as random events with very low probabilities, which happen nonetheless. He assumes that there is a huge number of planets where the conditions suitable for the formation of life are present, and hence that there is a substantial chance that at least on one of these planets (namely, Earth) an event will take place that cannot be explained by the natural selection mechanism, such as the origin of life itself – the appearance of the first living creature. Of course, this is a completely arbitrary assumption. But without getting into the arguments against this assumption, it is worth stressing, as we noted above, that in the framework of purely material evolution, it is impossible to explain the appearance of man and his spiritual qualities.

Let us summarize: *Dawkins' claim that the theory of natural selection explains evolution in general, including the appearance of man, in contrast to divine design which only "raises bigger questions", is incorrect, and the source of his mistake is his lack of understanding both of the nature of the development of life and of the Jewish view. In this book (Chapter Four) we saw that purely materialistic development is not sufficient to lead to numerous diverse creations. It is not possible to explain the evolution of life, as a whole, without providence. The evolution of life is part of the constantly renewing creation.*

5. *"The God Hypothesis suggests that the reality we inhabit also contains a supernatural agent who designed the universe and*

---

12. The origin of life, by contrast, lies outside the reach of that crane [the natural selection], because natural selection cannot proceed without it... [T]he origin of the eucaryotic cell (our kind of cell, with a nucleus and various other complicated features such as mitochondria, which are not present in bacteria) was an even more momentous, difficult and statistically improbable step than the origin of life. The origin of consciousness might be another major gap whose bridging was of the same order of improbability. (Ibid. p. 168)

— at least in many versions of the hypothesis — maintains it and even intervenes in it with miracles, which are temporary violations of his own otherwise grandly immutable laws." (pp. 81-82)

While the problem of miracles does not have a central place in the argument about the nature of the development of life, perhaps Dawkins' comment indicates a serious lack of understanding of the concept of divine guidance. And one cannot conduct an argument without understanding the view that is being criticized. Dawkins is certain that miracles, by definition, violate the principles of science.[13] The problem of miracles versus the laws of nature has a long-standing history. Does God, who determines the world order, Himself violate it? Does divine providence which operates constantly also "daily, perpetually" violate the laws of nature, which are the divine order? And on the human level: How is free will compatible with natural lawfulness, since all of man's limbs are material and their movements must be determined by the laws of nature? Immanuel Kant asked this question and could not come up with an answer, but he was not prepared to relinquish free will. Kant's problem was that he was relying on the deterministic physics of his time, and he was certain that it was the proven truth, but since then our understanding of the world of nature has progressed.

In fact, this problem lies at the heart of the discussion about the meaning of the world. Is it closed and develops on its own, according to the laws set from time immemorial, with no room for either providence or free will? Or is the material world, the world of nature, open both to the wills of man and to divine providence? It is worth noting that two important thinkers, Karl Popper (who defines himself as an agnostic) and John Eccles (who defines himself as a believer) held firmly to the openness of the world of nature to man's "Self", which is able to steer his body. From Dawkins'

---

13. Ibid. p. 83

point of view, the Self, with its free will, with its purposefulness and its emotions, does not exist at all and is simply an illusion. In Dawkins' closed, imaginary world, the laws of physics exclusively determine everything, and there is no room for free will. One must understand that such a view denies the existence of man as a creative entity who is responsible for his actions. In Chapter Two, section 6 we showed that the openness of the world to divine providence and the wills of man is compatible with the laws of physics and does not contradict them. Miracles, too, are compatible with the laws of physics.

In contrast with classical, deterministic physics, with which Kant was familiar, the laws of modern physics are non-deterministic and are compatible with the openness of the world to divine providence and man. The laws of nature are sufficiently flexible to "allow" the involvement of providence and man in the actions of matter, without violating these laws, in complete contrast to Dawkins' claims.

6. Dawkins' attitude to religion

A large part of Dawkins' book is dedicated to a negative and aggressive attitude towards all religions, and to an apologetic stance towards atheism. In Alister McGrath's book[14], there is a detailed and persuasive response to Dawkins' anti-religious arguments, based on his previous books. I do not intend to relate to this subject here – I only wish to add the following comment: Everything that is presented in Dawkins' book as the Jewish-religious view that is based on the Bible is nothing but a distortion of Judaism and a caricature of it. Dawkins completely ignores many generations of Biblical commentators and Jewish thinkers who have molded Judaism. *Dawkins' simplistic view of religion is entirely in keeping with his positions regarding God and the world, which we have discussed in this Appendix.*

---

14. Alister McGrath, *Dawkins' God: Genes, Memes, and the Meaning of Life*

Conclusion

I have discussed and responded to the main arguments that Dawkins brings to excuse his atheistic worldview. But the central claim from Dawkins' point of view can be summarized with the following quotation: "What most atheists do believe is that although there is only one kind of stuff in the universe and it is physical, out of this stuff come minds, beauty, emotions, moral values – in short the full gamut of phenomena that gives richness to human life."[15] This is Dawkins' belief, and as we have seen throughout this book and in the Appendix, this belief has no basis. It is precisely the kind of belief that can be referred to as "blind faith".

But Dawkins claims more than this. He claims that this is all supported by science. According to him, even the existence of God can be tested scientifically: "...the existence of God is a scientific hypothesis like any other."[16] And if it is impossible to prove or refute any belief, then the claim of the scientific nature of one view or another can both be criticized and refuted – and that is what has been done in the book that you are currently holding. The conclusion is that there is no scientific basis for Dawkins' atheistic belief – and nor is there any scientific study that supports his claim that "out of this stuff come minds, beauty, emotions, moral values". We have also seen that there is no scientific theory of the development of life on Earth. Furthermore, we have seen that purely material development, without providence, cannot be responsible for the appearance of the spiritual qualities that constitute the essence of man. In addition, Dawkins is certain that just as the theory of evolution "explains" the development of the animal kingdom, the creation of the species and the creation of man, another scientific theory in the future will be discovered that will explain the existence of law and order in the world. But despite Dawkins' hopes, there is no, and nor can there be any,

---

15. *The God Delusion*, p. 34
16. Ibid. p. 72

scientific explanation for the creation of the world and the existence of law and order in it – it does not belong to science, it simply is not within its jurisdiction.

To put it succinctly: *There is no basis, either scientific or rational, for Dawkins' atheistic view that is presented in his book,* The God Delusion.

BIBLIOGRAPHY

Armstrong David. M. A Materialist Theory of the Mind, London: Routledge & Kegan Paul, 1968.

Barrow, John D. & Frank J. Tipler. The Anthropic Cosmological Principle, Oxford: Oxford University Press, 1996.

Bell, John S. Speakable and Unspeakable in Quantum Mechanics, Cambridge: Cambridge University Press, 1993.

Ben Shlomo, Yosef. Lectures on the Philosophy of Spinoza. Translated by Shmuel Himelstein. Tel Aviv: Ministry of Defense, 1992.

Бен-Шломо, Йосеф. Введение в Философию Иудаизма, Тарбут, Иерусалим, 1994

Berkovits, Eliezer. Faith after the Holocaust. New York: Ktav Publishing House, 1973.

—. God, Man and History. Jerusalem: Shalem Press, 2004.

—. Essential Essays on Judaism. Jerusalem: Shalem Press, 2002.

Born, Max & Albert Einstein. The Born-Einstein Letters: Correspondence between Albert Einstein and Max and Hedwig Born from 1916 to 1955, with Commentaries by Max Born. London: Macmillan, 1971.

Buber, Martin. I and Thou. New York: Collier Books, 1958.

Burtt, Edwin A. The Metaphysical Foundations of Modern Science. Atlantic Highlands, N. J.: Humanities Press, 1996.

Carmell, Aryeh & Cyril Domb, Eds. Challenge: Torah Views on Science and Its Problems. New York: Feldheim, 1978.

Darwin, Charles. On the Origin of Species. London: John Murray, 1859; New York: Bantam Classics, 1999.

Descartes, René. Key Philosophical Writings. Hertfordshire: Wordsworth Classics, 1997.

Dessler, Rabbi Eliyahu. Strive For Truth. Translated from the Hebrew (Michtav Me-eliyahu) by Aryeh Carmell. Jerusalem/NewYork: Feldheim, 1978.

Einstein, Albert. Ideas and Opinions. New York: Wings Books, 1954.

—. & Leopold Infeld. Evolution of Physics. Cambridge: Cambridge University Press, 1938.

Fackenheim, Emil L. God's Presence in History. New York: New York University Press, 1970.

—. Quest for Past and Future, Boston: Beacon Press, 1968.

—. The Jewish Return into History: Reflection in the Age of Auschwitz and a New Jerusalem. New York: Schocken Books, 1978.

—. What Is Judaism? New York: Summit Books, 1987.

—. To Mend the World, New York: Schocken Books, 1982.

Fain, Benjamin. "Comprehensibility of the World: Jewish Outlook." BDD [Bekhol Derakhekha Deahu] Journal of Torah and Scholarship, 9: 5-21.

—. Creation Ex Nihilo, Jerusalem/New York: Gefen, 2007.

—. Вера и Разум, Маханаим, Иерусалим, 2007.

—. Evolution and Providence, in Divine Action and Natural Selection (Eds: J. Seckbach and R. Gordon), New Jersey/Singapore: World Scientific, 2009.

—. Irreversibilities in Quantum Mechanics. Dordrecht, Netherlands: Kluwer Academic Publishers, 2000. (See specifically chapter 6, "Quantum Measurement and Irreversibility.")

—. & Mervin F. Verbit. Jewishness in the Soviet Union: Report of an Empirical Survey. Jerusalem: Jerusalem Center for Public Affairs/ Tarbut, 1984.

—. Law and Providence, Jerusalem/New York: Urim Publications, 2011.

Feynman, Richard. The Character of Physical Law. London: Cox and Wyman Ltd, 1965.

Feynman, Richard, Robert B. Leighton & Matthew Sands. The Feynman Lectures on Physics, Vol.1. London: Addison-Wesley, 1963.

Fukuyama, Francis. The End of History and the Last Man. London: Penguin Books, 1993.

Galilei, Galileo. Dialogue Concerning the Two Chief World Systems. Berkley: University of California Press, 1953.

—. Two New Sciences: Including Centers of Gravity & Force of Percussion. Madison, Wis.: University of Wisconsin Press, 1974.

Gödel, Kurt. On Formally Undecidable Propositions of Principia Mathematica and Related Systems. Translated by B. Meltzer. New York: Basic Books, 1962.

Gould, Stephen J. Wonderful Life: The Burgess Shale and the Nature of History. London: Penguin Books, 1989.

Greene, Brian. The Elegant Universe: Superstrings, Hidden Dimensions, and the Quest for the Ultimate Theory. New York: W. W. Norton, 1999.

Guttmann, Julius. Philosophies of Judaism. Translated by David Silverman. New York: Schocken Books, 1973.

Heschel, Abraham J. Between God and Man: an Interpretation of Judaism. London: The Free Press, 1959.

—. The Wisdom of Heschel. Translated by Ruth M. Goodhill. New York: Farrar, Strauss and Giroux: 1975

Hume, David. The Natural History of Religion and Dialogues concerning Natural Religion. Oxford: Clarendon Press, 1976.

—. A Treatise of Human Nature. Edited by L. A. Selby-Bigge. Oxford: Clarendon Press, 1888. (Russian translation- 1996)

Johnson, Paul. A History of the Jews. New York: Harper Perennial, 1988.

Kant, Immanuel. Critique of Practical Reason. Chicago: University of Chicago Press, 1949.

—. Critique of Pure Reason. London: Macmillan, 1923.

—. Prolegomena to Any Future Metaphysics. New York: Liberal Arts Press, 1950.

Kolitz, Zvi. Confrontation. Hoboken, New Jersey: Ktav, 1993.

Levi, Yehudah. Torah and Science. Jerusalem/New York: Feldheim Publishers, 2006.

Lucas John R.: The Freedom of the Will, Oxford: Clarendon Press, 1970.

Luzzatto, Rabbi Moshe Chaim. The Way of God. Translated by Arieh Kaplan. Jerusalem: Feldheim, 1983.

Maimonides, Moses. The Guide of the Perplexed. 2 vols. Translated by Shlomo Pines. Chicago: University of Chicago Press, 1963.

Mayr, Ernst. One Long Argument: Charles Darwin and the Genesis of Modern Evolutionary Thought. Cambridge MA: Harvard University Press, 1993.

Monod, Jacques. Chance and Necessity: An Essay on the Natural Philosophy of Modern Biology. London: Penguin Books, 1997.

Nagel, Ernest & James R. Newman. Goedel's Proof. New York: New York University Press, 1958.

Newton, Isaac. Optics. New York: Dover, 1952.

Penfield, Wilder. The Mystery of the Mind. Princeton: Princeton University Press, 1975.

Penrose, Roger. The Emperor's New Mind: Concerning Computers, Minds and The Laws of Physics. London: Vintage, 1990.

Popper, Karl R. Conjectures and Refutations. London: Routledge, 2000.

—. Knowledge and the Body-Mind Problem. London: Routledge, 2000.

—. The Logic of Scientific Discovery. London: Routledge, 1992.

—. Objective Knowledge: An Evolutionary Approach. Oxford: Clarendon Press, 1981.

—. The Open Society and Its Enemies. Vol. 1, The Spell of Plato. Vol. 2, The High Tide of Prophesy: Hegel, Marx, and the Aftermath. London: Routledge, 1999.

—. The Open Universe. London: Routledge, 1995.

—. The Poverty of Historicism. London: Routledge, 1999.

—. Quantum Theory and the Schism in Physics. London: Routledge, 1995.

—. Realism and the Aim of Science. London: Routledge, 1994.

—. Unended Quest. London: Routledge, 1993.

—. & John C. Eccles. The Self and Its Brain. London: Routledge, 1995.

Russell, Bertrand. A History of Western Philosophy. New York: Simon and Schuster, 1945.

—. Human Knowledge: Its Scope and Limits. London: George Allen and Unwin, 1948.

Schilpp, Paul A., Ed. Albert Einstein: Philosopher-Scientist, the Library of Living Philosophers. New York: Tudor Publishing, 1951.

Scholem, Gershom. Major Trends in Jewish Mysticism. Jerusalem: Schocken, 1941.

Schrödinger, Erwin. Mind and Matter. Cambridge: Cambridge University Press, 1961.

—. What Is Life? Cambridge: Cambridge University Press, 1948.

Simpson, George G. The Meaning of Evolution. New York: New American Library, 1951.

Soloveitchik, Rabbi Joseph B. And From There You Shall Seek. Translated from the Hebrew by Naomi Goldblum. New York: Ktav Publishing House, 2008.

—. Halakhic Man. Philadelphia: Jewish Publication Society of America, 1983.

—. Halakhic Mind. London: Collier Macmillan Publishers, 1986.

—. Fate and destiny: From Holocaust to the State of Israel. Translation of Kol Dodi Dofek by L. Kaplan. Hoboken, N. J.: Ktav Publishing House, 2000

Westfall, Richard S. Never at Rest. A Biography of Isaac Newton. Cambridge: Cambridge University Press, 1980.

Whitehead, Alfred N. Adventures of Ideas. New York: The Free Press, 1961.

—. Science and the Modern World. New York: Macmillan, 1935.

Wigner, Eugene. The Unreasonable Effectiveness of Mathematics in the Natural Sciences in Commun. on Pure and Appl. Math., XIII, 3. New York: John Wiley and Sons, 1960.

In Hebrew

Agassi, Yosef. Toldot ha-filosofiah ha-chadashah [The history of modern philosophy]. Tel Aviv: Tel Aviv University, 1993.

Aviner, Rabbi Shlomo. Sefer ha-kuzari: Perush [The Kuzari: A commentary]. Bet-El: Sifriat Chava, 2003-2007.

Ben Shlomo, Yosef. "Shirat ha-chaim": Prakim be-mishnato shel ha-Rav Kook [Song of life: Selections from the teachings of R. Kook]. Tel Aviv: The Ministry of Defense, 1989.

Berkovitzs, Eliezer. Maamarim al yesodot hayadut [Essays on the foundations of Judaism] (in Russian). Jerusalem: Shalem Press, 1994.

Buber, Martin. Be-sod siyach [In the secret of dialogue]. Jerusalem: Mossad Bialik, 1959.

Dessler, Rabbi Eliyahu. Michtav Me-eliyahu [Letter from Eliyahu]. Tel Aviv: Sifriati, 1995.

Eldad, Israel. Hegionot yisrael [Reflections on Israel]. Tel Aviv: Hamidrasha Haleumit/Yair, 1980.

Fain, Benjamin. Evolutziah shel ha-chayim [The evolution of life]. Asia, Issue 77-78, January 2006, 38-64.

—. Yesh me'ayin: Machshevot al Hamada, hahashgacha haelyona, habechira hachofshit, haemuna and chavayat chayai. [Creation ex nihilo: thoughts on science, divine providence, free will, faith and the experiences of my life]. Jerusalem: Reuven Mass, 2004; Mechon Har Bracha, 2008

—. Hok ve'hashgakha [Law and providence]. Jerusalem: Mechon Har Bracha, 2009.

Halevi, Rabbi Yehuda ben Shmuel. Ha-Kuzari. Be-ha'takato shel Rabbi Yehuda Ibn Tibbon [The Kuzari: translated by Rabbi Yehuda Ibn Tibbon]. Tel Aviv: Hamenorah, 1984.

Maimon, Solomon. Ha-masah al ha-filosofiah ha-transzendentalit [Essay on transcendental philosophy]. Translated and edited by Shmuel H. Bergman and Nathan Rottenstreich. Jerusalem: Hebrew University, 1941.

Maimonides, Moses. Hakdamot le-perush ha-mishneh, hakdamah lemasechet avot [Introduction to the commentary on the Mishneh, introduction to Ethics of our Fathers]. Jeruslaem: Mossad HaRav Kook. 1961.

Scholem, Gershom. Devarim be-go [Explications and implications]. Tel Aviv: Am Oved, 1990.

Schweid, Eliezer. Ha-filosofim ha-gedolim shelanu [Our great philosophers]. Tel Aviv: Yediot Aharonot, 1999.

—.Toldot filosofiat ha-dat ha-yehudit b'zman h-hadash [The history of the philosophy of the Jewish religion in modern times]. Volumes 1-4. Tel Aviv: Am Oved, 2001-2006.

Shalit, Daniel. Eretz Shamayim [Land of Heaven]. Jerusalem: Tavai, 2009.

Shwartz, Moshe. Mimitos lehitgalut [From myth to revelation]. Tel Aviv: Hotzaat Hakibbutz Hameuchad, 1978.

Soloveitchik, Rabbi Joseph B. Ha-adam ve-olamo [Man and his world]. Jerusalem: Eliner Library Department of religious Education and Culture in the Diaspora, 1998.

—. Ish ha-emunah [Man of Faith]. Jerusalem: Mossad HaRav Kook, 1992.

—. Ish ha-halakhah: Galui ve-nistar [Halakhic man: revealed and hidden]. Jeruslaem: Hahistadrut Hatzionit Haolamit, 1992 (See specifically "U-Vikashtem misham" [And from there shall you seek]).